The Psychic World of
DEREK ACORAH

The Psychic World of
DEREK ACORAH

Derek Acorah
with John G. Sutton

PIATKUS

First published in 1999 by
Judy Piatkus (Publishers) Ltd
5 Windmill Street, London W1T 2JA
email: info@piatkus.co.uk

For more information on other books published by Piatkus,
visit our website at *www.piatkus.co.uk*

Reprinted 2000 (twice), 2001 (twice)

The moral rights of the authors have been asserted

A catalogue record for this book is available from the British Library

ISBN 0-7499-2024-6

Typeset by Action Publishing Technology Ltd, Gloucester
Printed and bound in Great Britain by
The Bath Press, Bath

Contents

PART 2
The Essential Guide to
Developing Your Hidden Powers 81

PART 3
The Spiritual Dimension 147

This book is dedicated, with all my love, to my dear wife Gwen, without whom there would have been no book and perhaps no Derek Acorah

Acknowledgements

The author wishes to acknowledge the help and
assistance of the following:

Mr John G. Sutton, the writer whose tireless
dedication enabled me to create this book. Contact
John on the internet at www.PsychicWorld.net.
Dr Larry Montz, who tested and approved my
psychic powers at the ISPR (International Society for
Paranormal Research) HQ in Hollywood, CA, USA.
www.ispr.net
Mrs Mary Sutton, for services above and beyond the
call of duty.
Mrs Lois J. Barin MA of Columbus, Ohio, USA, for
her always constructive critique of the work in draft
form.
The Joe Cooper MSc BSc (Econ.) for his advice and
the continuous wearing of a very wrinkly, soup-
stained shirt.

Introduction

My name is Derek Acorah and I, like you, am a child of God. I know that God loves you as He loves all His children. I am a spirit medium and since I was a child I have been able to communicate with discarnate spirits alive in the world beyond this material plane that we call the earth. Within this book I will try to explain how I perceive the truth of life eternal. There is no such thing as death; we are all eternal beings incarnate in physical bodies. When those bodies die, we step out of them into the next world.

I offer the reader only that which I sincerely and honestly believe to be true. There is no need to be afraid of the truth. This truth should set you free to live your earthly life in peace and understanding, secure in the certain knowledge that you are the master of your own fate. For it is how you live this life that will determine your destiny in the kingdom of God that is to come. You are creating your own eternity. By your actions, your thoughts and deeds you will be judged, not by an old bearded man on a throne, but by yourself.

The book is divided into three sections. In the first part I tell my story and how I discovered my spiritual self, then denied it and became a football player with the famous Bill Shankly at Liverpool Football Club. My gift of mediumship has always been with me and I eventually recognised my destiny and accepted the path that I had prepared for myself long before I was born. I hope that this book will help you to recognise your true pathway to God.

Above all, this book is aimed at all those who are seeking to know the truth that is all around and within them. In the second section of this book I have created a series of tests and step-by-step tutorials to enable you, the reader, to assess and develop your own psychic potential. We are all gifted with hidden paranormal powers that can be awakened. I believe it is your God-given right to discover the truth for yourself.

In the final section, I offer the reader my personal insights into the work of mediums and our destiny in the psychic world beyond. When we are born we all carry the keys to the kingdom of God within ourselves. However, most of us have misplaced them on the road through this frequently difficult life. I sincerely hope this book, which is my truth, helps you to find your key to open the door into the light of eternal understanding.

My thoughts are with you.

PART 1

MY STORY

My Early
Psychic Experiences

As a child I lived with my parents in my grandmother's house in Brazennose Road, Bootle, on the outskirts of Liverpool. Our family name was Johnson but I always felt that mine should be Acorah. That was my gran's name when she was married to her first husband, who was a sailor born in the Netherlands. Gran said the name was favourable in numerology, relating to the Sun and the beginning of all things. Our family had a long history of spirit mediums and psychically gifted individuals within it. These were, before myself, always women. My gifts were recognised quite early by my gran. She herself was a medium and encouraged me to try and develop them.

However, I wanted to be a professional football player, and followed that path for a time. This is the story of how I discovered that, no matter how hard I tried to be something else, a medium is what I was born to be.

THE BROKEN WINDOW

As a child in the 1950s, I had a friend called Ricky Jones who lived just down the road from our house in Brazennose Road.

One day when we were about seven years old, he and I were kicking an old leather football in the road, as children do. I booted it to him and Ricky booted it back. There seemed no harm in our play, until Ricky kicked the ball hard against the railings outside his own house. The ball bounced up and smashed the front window.

Ricky didn't hesitate; he picked up his feet and ran. I stood there looking blankly at the broken window and wondering what we could say. I soon got the chance to find out.

The front door of Ricky's house flew open and out marched the five foot nothing of dynamite that was Mrs Jones. 'You little terror!' she yelled, gripping me by my right arm and twisting it. 'You'll pay for breaking my window!' she said and dragged me along Brazennose Road to my home.

'Your Derek's smashed our window with a football,' Mrs Jones told my granny when she opened the door. 'He'll have to pay, you know.'

I just looked at the floor.

My gran couldn't really argue with Mrs Jones, so she took her purse out of her apron pocket and gave her the cash to have the window replaced. 'No spending money for you for a while!' gran said to me as I dodged inside the house, ducking to avoid the hand she aimed at my head.

Although it was only afternoon, I was sent upstairs to bed in disgrace. I hated that! The other children were out playing while all I could do was watch them from the window of my bedroom. I saw little Ricky; he was running about with two older boys from round the corner. I had never liked them and I felt really angry inside that my friend had let me take the blame and then gone off to play with children I disliked. It didn't seem fair, but you didn't tell on your mates. So I took my punishment.

Looking out down Brazennose Road, I saw the glazier fitting the new front window in Mrs Jones's house. I'd have to pay for that out of my spending money. For a brief moment I hated that window and that nasty Mrs Jones. My arm still hurt from the twisting she gave it.

It took me hours to get to sleep. I could hear children laughing and singing as they played in the streets. Long into that hot August night I heard their calls, but I couldn't join them, because Ricky had broken a window.

The next day was a Sunday and I woke to the sun shining through the floral-patterned curtains and the seagulls calling in the cloudless sky. 'Your breakfast's ready, Derek!' Gran called, and I was downstairs almost before she'd finished speaking.

'Can I go out today, Gran, can I, please?' I asked between mouthfuls of toast and strawberry jam.

She looked at me in the way grannies do when they feel sorry for you. 'Derek,' she said, 'have you got something to tell me?' Well, my gran was psychic so she must have known.

'Yes,' I answered. 'It was Ricky who broke that window.'

For a moment Gran looked at me. 'I knew it!' she said. 'You see, Derek, during the night someone – or something – smashed Mrs Jones's new window.'

We never found out who or what broke that window on the night of my undeserved punishment. Looking back on the incident, I think it likely that my spirit guides had seen Mrs Jones hurting and blaming me for something I didn't do. Perhaps they intervened to teach her a lesson.

FACES IN THE DOOR

When I was about eight, I had what I now know to be a series of visions. At the time they scared me just a little.

It began in the late afternoon of one dark November day. Gran's house had just been fitted with an indoor toilet and it was newly painted in some glossy shade of blue. I was sitting there looking at the back of the door and thinking how shiny it was. Then I saw a face and thought it didn't look much like me. Suddenly I realised that this was not in fact a reflection; this was something else.

The face was looking back at me, its eyes shining and gentle. It was the face of an old man with thick grey hair and a funny beard. He seemed to know me and smiled in a way that filled me with joy. Then he vanished and another face appeared. This time I saw a mature lady with long dark hair and the happiest eyes I ever did see. This lady's face was glowing. I felt overcome with delight at seeing these people, as though they were my long-lost friends.

One by one, new images appeared on the toilet door. As a new one popped up, the previous one floated into the air and disappeared over my head. I can still visualise that amazing experience.

Before I fell asleep that night, I was under the bedcovers pretending to be a Native American in a tent. As I lay there dreaming about cowboys and the Wild West, I felt someone large come and sit on the bottom of my bed. No one else was in the room, and I had heard no one open the bedroom door. I didn't feel scared, just wondered who it might be.

Slowly whatever or whoever it was edged up my bed closer towards me. Then I began to feel a strange tingling sensation all around my head and shoulders. Gradually this spread down my body to my chest. It was the most glorious sensation I had ever experienced. It felt as though I were being bathed in a golden light of pure love. I nearly sang out in delight.

Almost in ecstasy, I threw the sheets off me and felt power flooding through my body. I was a man, I was a strong man, now I was an adult! Oh, I was so proud of my long muscular arms and heavy chest! The sense of manhood and pride surged through me. Then I heard a voice I almost recognised saying, 'Be calm, my son, be peaceful, we are with you, we are your guides and we love you. Now and for always we will walk beside you.'

I cried out in absolute happiness. Tears of divine joy ran down my face and I wept for the love I felt filling me from my head to my toes.

Another voice said, 'We are your family. Think how fortunate you are, you are our child.'

And then the night closed in quietly around me and they

were gone. Gone back into a world I did not understand and could not reach. For a moment I felt abandoned, alone. Then sleep overtook me until once again it was morning in Bootle and Gran was calling me down for breakfast.

After the toast and cornflakes I dared to tell Gran what I had seen and how I had felt. Taking my hand in hers, she just smiled in that special way she had when she was going to tell me something important. 'Those were your spirit guides,' she said. 'Whenever you need to be strong, they will stand beside you.' And then she gave me a piece of her home-made treacle tart as a special treat. I hoped those spirit guides would call again soon; my gran's treacle tart was the best in Bootle.

THE STIGMATIC CHILD

My granny was always being asked to help people in our area who were experiencing supernatural or inexplicable happenings. In those days, most folk seemed to believe in spirits and ghosts. I suppose it was because many families had suffered losses in the Second World War and wanted to think their loved ones lived on. There were not many homes with TV sets then, at least not down our street, and often groups would meet to hold a seance. Gran, being a well-known medium, was in great demand. When she sat in a circle, something was certain to happen.

Sometimes Gran would take me with her on her visits to the neighbours' houses. One day she took me along to the home of a very sick young girl. I was only nine years old and Gran told me to wait in the living room of this house while she went upstairs. After what seemed like an hour, but was more likely about ten minutes, I got bored. There was nothing to do in the room, nothing to read even, so I wandered up the stairs.

From the landing outside the little girl's room, I looked in and saw what I thought was a pool of blood. I could see my

gran sitting at the side of the bed, but the girl was hidden
from me by what appeared to be a cloud of bright red blood
that was floating over her.

Hearing my footsteps, Gran turned and saw me. Her eyes
were glowing as though lit by some internal fire. 'What do
you see, Derek?' she said. The words washed over me and I
struggled to decipher their meaning. 'Derek, tell me what
you see,' she said.

My mouth opened and closed but my tongue would not
move. I was unable to speak. Seconds that felt like hours
passed and I stared in dumbstruck horror at the oozing red
blanket of blood that drifted over the body of the little girl.
Then it cleared, as though something unseen had changed
the picture before me. I looked and now saw the child. She
was thin and frail but her face was heavenly. 'She is an angel,
Gran! You're sitting with an angel!' Gran's eyes shone
brightly as I spoke. 'Soon she will be with God,' I said, and
trembled as the words passed my lips.

Why I had said that I did not know. But my granny smiled
as she held the limp and almost lifeless hand of that sick little
girl. 'So you do see the spirit world, my boy!' she said. And I
have been able to 'see' it from that day onwards.

Back home that afternoon, I told Gran all that I had seen.
Gran explained to me then that she thought I had a very
special gift that one day would bring much peace and understanding to the world. But I didn't understand. I just wanted
to know why I saw all that blood. In truth it frightened me,
for I was just a child.

'The little girl is indeed an angel,' Gran said. 'The blood
you saw is a sign from the world beyond that she is of the
Blood. Derek, the girl you saw today is a stigmatic.' You can
imagine that word baffled me. 'Her body displays wounds
that bleed like the wounds inflicted on Our Lord Jesus
Christ during his crucifixion,' Gran explained.

I knew the family of that little girl, they were devout
Catholics. The next week that little girl passed into spirit. It
was all too much for me then. How could I 'see' things that

were not really there? My granny wouldn't tell me lies, but why me?

Almost forty years have come and gone since that long-ago day when I saw the blood. Since then I have encountered many angels and many spirits that were far from angelic. But no matter how often I see the visitors from beyond the grave, I shall never forget that first encounter with the angel of death, when my inner eyes were opened to the next dimension.

FROZEN FISH

Gran would often send me to the shops to get groceries – potatoes, tea, that kind of thing. Down our street there was a corner shop, but a little further along, just round the corner, there was a butcher's and a baker's and a wet-fish shop. I used to go to the fish shop every Friday around noon with Gran's order; I suppose it was haddock or plaice for the Friday dinner. I always carried the money in a little purse Gran handed me with her written order. 'Run straight there and back, our Derek,' she would say, and off I'd go.

In those days the fish came off the docks almost frozen solid and was kept packed in ice at the fishmonger's. I'd hand the order to the fishmonger along with Gran's purse, and receive the fish wrapped in paper. It was always freezing cold when I grabbed hold of it, and I would run straight back to our house where Gran was waiting. But no matter how quickly I ran, and the distance was no more than five hundred yards or so, the fish was always defrosted and warm by the time I got there.

At first Gran thought I'd been messing about with the fish, but I hadn't. She knew I must have run there and back because I'd been gone only a few minutes. So she pondered on the mystery of the fish. Though I was only a child of about eight, I too knew something fishy was going on.

One day, after I had once again returned with warm fish, Gran called me into her front room and sat me down. She placed her hands on my hands, palms upwards, and looked into the far corner of the room, smiling in a funny kind of way, as if there was someone there.

'You know, our Derek,' she said, 'You're a special child.' I thought she meant because I did the shopping, but she didn't. 'You were once a healing spirit and have that gift within you.'

It was beyond me at the time. But I know now why the fish became defrosted in my hands. The healing energy within me was discharging itself through the palms of my hands. I was developing as a medium and the forces beyond were opening my channels.

In later years Gran would often remind me of the warm fish and tell me that she had seen a vision on that day of my previous life as a healer. In that previous life I had fallen from grace and used my powers for gain and self-glorification. When Gran told me that, I made her a promise: it might have happened before but it was not going to happen again. And it won't. My gifts are too precious to be thrown away for a fleeting moment of fame. My gifts are meant to bring the truth to the world and nothing less.

From the day of Gran's vision onwards, I always went to the fishmonger's with a little string bag. And the fish arrived home still packed in ice and as fresh as when it had left the docks.

SCALLYWAG PARK

One of my hobbies when I was about ten was to watch birds along the canal near our house. Often there were three of us, my school friends Vinny and Frank and I. We competed against each other, seeing who could spot the first mallard or robin. We never counted sparrows, though. The area was full of sparrows, all coughing in the city smoke. There was no nature park round Bootle where I lived, but with sunshine reflecting off the canal and a warm summer breeze ruffling the smoke from the distant factory chimneys, we didn't really care. To us Liverpool lads it was better than some snooty zoo – this was ours, this was Scallywag Park.

One day we'd marched all the way up the canal towpath and were not far from the Melling Road, made famous by the Grand National horse race run at Aintree course. It was late afternoon and, apart from a bag of crisps between us, we'd had nothing to eat since breakfast. It was time to turn back and run home for dinner.

I was always the fastest, and was yards ahead when I saw a group of boys I knew. 'Get an ambulance!' they shouted. 'Go get Tony's mum!' called one boy I knew from school.

As soon as I heard those words I began to feel ill. A dreadful pain shot through my side and I clutched at my stomach. 'I'll be OK,' I said out loud. 'Going to be fine.' I did not know at the time why I said that. But I did know that someone very close by had been injured.

We sent Vinny, who was quite nippy and knew where the boy called Tony lived. Then Frank and I ran along with the other boys to see what had happened. My stomach and back were still hurting but in my mind I felt quite certain that whoever had been hurt would survive.

As we turned a corner into a farmer's field, I saw the horror of what had happened. The boy, Tony, was impaled on the top of a spiked fence of iron railings. One had entered through his lower back and the jagged end was protruding through his stomach wall. Blood dribbled slowly from this open wound and fell to the ground below. Tony had been climbing in the tree overhanging this rusty old fence and had slipped off a branch. He was crying now, a whimpering sound that sent shivers of fear tingling up my back.

The fence was about six feet high and we could hardly reach him. There seemed to be nothing we could do for him.

Then I heard myself speaking. Yet it wasn't my voice, it was someone else speaking through me. 'Tony,' I said, 'believe me, you're going to live. Keep perfectly still, help will be here soon.' And I reached up and managed to touch his brow. It was cold and clammy, he was in shock. I knew he needed to be kept awake. 'Talk to me, Tony!' I shouted. 'You'll live, I'm telling you!'

I sensed someone by me, some invisible being giving me the strength I needed. I held his hand and talked of football, of our heroes on the playing fields of Liverpool and Everton. Somehow, I was not afraid.

Suddenly there was a nurse and an ambulance driver beside me. They lifted poor Tony off that awful spike and carried his limp body away to hospital. 'You're a brave young man!' one of the nurses said. 'Who taught you to be so strong?'

I could hardly tell her the truth so I said, 'Oh, me gran.' And in a way that was the truth.

Tony did survive, though it took weeks of intensive care and months of rehabilitation. I expect he's out there somewhere today living his life to the full, just as I knew he would be, all those years ago when I was just a little boy running wild in Scallywag Park.

My Spiritual Awakening

VISITATION ON THE FOOTBALL PITCH

I was ten and a half years old and the captain of my junior school's football team. The Merseyside area team selectors had been to see me play and picked me for the Bootle Boys side. The competition for places on this team was intense, but I had scored many goals over the season in my position of inside right. Whenever I aimed and kicked the ball, it seemed to find the net.

Our side had been drawn to play an away game against one of the very best teams in the area, the Huyton Boys Under Thirteens. To a ten-year-old, a thirteen-year-old boy can seem more like a grown man, and Huyton Boys were a tough lot, noted for their crippling tackles. To complete a game against them in one piece was hard enough. I wasn't big for my age, but I was very fast with almost magical feet. I was going to need them.

My mum insisted on coming with me to the match. At that age children don't want Mummy holding their hand, but mine wouldn't let me go alone. I think Gran put her up to it, thinking I might need some support. We arrived at the dressing rooms at the side of the football pitch in Huyton at least an hour before the match. I felt a right chump sitting there with Mummy straightening my shirt and combing my hair.

The first half of this football match was a real struggle. Some of those Huyton Boys were huge and they were pushing and shoving me every time I got anywhere near the ball. In truth, they really were a far superior side and too powerful for us. At half-time we were losing the match 3–0.

Sitting in the dressing room listening to our coach telling the team how to avoid being slaughtered, I had a vision. Suddenly I saw myself out on the pitch, and our goalkeeper, Mike Rawlinson, was lying flat on the ground. I could see he had been badly injured. In my mind I heard the coach say, 'Mike can no longer take part in this game, who will volunteer to take his position?' Then the scene in my mind changed and I saw myself standing in the goal wearing the keeper's green jersey. This was highly improbable as I was perhaps the smallest player on the pitch and goalkeepers are usually the biggest.

This fleeting vision passed and it was time for the team to take the field for the second half. Mum gave me a little hug and adjusted my shirt.

The match was less than five minutes into the second half when I heard a terrible scream behind me. Turning, I saw that Mike, our goalkeeper, was on the ground howling in agony. One of the Huyton team had kicked him in his most sensitive parts. Mike had to be carried from the field and taken to hospital by ambulance.

'Mike can no longer take part in this game, who will volunteer to take his position?' the coach said. It was the scene exactly as I had 'seen' it in the dressing room.

In my mind I heard a voice saying, 'You do it, son, you do it, Derek, we're with you, we'll help.' So I volunteered.

Now, being a football goalkeeper is something I had never been any good at. I was far too small. The others openly laughed. However, no one else wanted to be goalkeeper so the coach threw me the green jersey, and I was in goal.

How was I going to cope with those big Huyton boys booting the ball at me? Strangely, as I stood in that goal, I began to feel bigger and stronger. I was a real goalkeeper and I played like one, making save after brilliant save. My confidence grew with each minute that passed. Our supporters were going wild, shouting and dancing on the touch line. My mum was waving a team scarf over her head. Our side took heart and began to attack the big Huyton boys. Then we scored! The game was 3–1 to Huyton but we were moving forward and making ground. We scored again, it was 3–2 now and they did not like that one little bit. I could see the anger in their eyes as they lined up to restart the game after that score.

It was more like a battle charge from Huyton now as they hurled everything they had at our much smaller team. Then the referee blew his whistle. From where I stood between our goalposts I could just make out the body of one of our team players writhing on the ground. The referee called it foul play and awarded a penalty kick against Huyton Boys. As the injured player had been our usual penalty taker, the coach had to select another to take the kick. I was nominated.

As I walked forward to face the big keeper in Huyton's goal, I felt a hand on my shoulder. Thinking it was our team captain, I turned, but there was no one there. I felt calm then, as though that gentle touch had steadied my nerves. In my mind a voice I faintly recognised said, 'Hit it hard, my son, we are with you.'

I just ran up, kicked the ball and scored: 3–3 even and the match was almost over. I could see my mum jumping up and down at the side of the pitch.

And that was how the game ended – a draw. The team lifted me up on their shoulders and ran me round the field. It was a brilliant experience but I knew I hadn't done it alone. My friends in the world of spirit had been there alongside me.

As I walked back into the dressing room, I heard the voice again: 'You were brave, son, you acted with courage. Whenever you need us, we will be with you. You will never walk alone.' I was almost overcome with joy as I heard those wonderful words and I couldn't wait to get home and tell Gran what had happened.

A VICTORY FOR BOOTLE BOYS

By the age of thirteen I was playing football for the senior youth team in our area, also called Bootle Boys. I was one of the youngest members and my school games master told me he thought I would be a professional player in time. I just loved football and my father encouraged me all the way. He was a lifelong supporter of Everton FC and I accompanied him to many home games at Goodison Park where Everton played. There were two top teams in the Merseyside area; Liverpool, managed by the legendary Bill Shankly, and Everton. If I could play for either side as a professional, then I would be an instant local hero.

The Bootle Boys team I now played for was attracting attention from football scouts. We were winning lots of games and scoring plenty of goals. I had been on good form in my favourite position, inside right. A scout from Wrexham FC asked my parents if I would go to their ground in Wales to discuss the idea of signing up as an apprentice. 'Well done, our Derek!' Gran shouted at the top of her voice when I told her.

All the way to Wrexham I was really nervous. Mum was with me and Dad was driving our old Ford Anglia. I thought that this was my big chance and I had better not miss it. I had my favourite boots and my best kit in a new duffel bag. We had brought sandwiches and home-made treacle tart, and were all set for a good day out.

It was a brilliant day. As I sat in the dressing room of Wrexham FC getting changed into my football kit, I felt a by now familiar invisible presence alongside me. A voice I recognised spoke in my mind. 'Do your best, son,' it said. 'We're with you.'

Out on the pitch I ran the socks off the full-time professionals of Wrexham FC. They just couldn't catch me. By the time I had finished, the manager himself was out on the touch line watching the game. I came away with a contract as an apprentice. When I told my gran, she nearly cried with joy.

From then on I was training at school, playing for Bootle Boys at weekends, and often I would train at night too. I was determined to be a professional and wanted to be the very best.

One day I woke early. All through the night I had been drifting in and out of sleep and had not rested properly. At 8 a.m. I set off to school but, unusually for me, I didn't want to go. I felt heavy, ill at ease and strangely sad.

It was 11.30 a.m. and I had just completed an English lesson in which the teacher had been reading poetry to the class. I loved poetry, which my friends thought odd in a football player. It seemed to touch my soul and raise my spirits that day, but then the deputy headmaster came into the classroom and called me out. He said the headmaster himself wanted to see me. For a second I wondered what I had done. Smoking behind the bike sheds? I didn't think anyone knew about that.

As the door to the headmaster's office opened, I saw my mother sitting in a chair crying. I knew instantly what she was going to say. 'Gran died this morning, Derek.'

Gran had gone! She who had always been there for me when I had needed help was no more. It really broke my heart.

I insisted on being taken to see her for one last time. I had to say a final farewell to the one person in this world who had understood me. In a little room at Walton General Hospital her body was lying on a bed. I took her old hand in mine and thought of the many times she had comforted me as a boy. Without her guidance I know I would never have accepted my gifts.

Some nights later, as I lay in my bed quietly crying for the lost love of my dear gran, I became aware of a beautiful fragrance filling the room. The scent was of wallflowers. These had been Gran's favourites and I knew immediately that in spirit she was with me. Then I slipped into sleep and in my dreams she was alive; she would always be alive, and I will never, ever forget her.

It was with a heavy heart that I returned to playing football, but I was improving all the time. Bootle Boys football team had their best season, we even got to the final of the local W. R. Williams Cup. Our opponents were the red-hot favourites Liverpool Schoolboys. Everyone said they would beat us easily.

I scored a great goal that day. When I received the ball there were three, maybe four, players defending the goal in front of me. Somehow I shot round them and booted the ball into the back of the net. Our supporters went wild with delight. We Bootle Boys won 3–0. The final was played on the pitch at Anfield, home of Liverpool FC.

Watching that match were some of England's top football-team managers. Among them were Bill Shankly and Tommy Docherty. After the game was over, Bill Shankly came up to me and shook my hand. 'Och, lad,' he said in his Scottish brogue, 'you'll be signing for my team now.' I tried to tell Mr Shankly that I was already signed to Wrexham FC but he didn't seem to hear me.

Within two days an agent from Shankly's Liverpool FC was at our house with a contract for my parents to sign on my behalf. When Dad asked him about Wrexham, he just smiled and said, 'Mr Shankly sorted that out the day your lad scored against Liverpool Schoolboys. Just sign here.' And we did!

PLAYING FOR LIVERPOOL FC

And so, at only fifteen, I found myself an apprentice foot-
baller signed to Liverpool FC. The year was 1965 and the
Liverpool team were at the very top of the First Division of
the Football League. It is hard to believe, looking back, but
every single first-team player at the club had been selected
and capped as a player for their country. I was in awe of the
first-team players and as for the manager, Bill Shankly, he
was my hero. In fact, Bill Shankly was every football player's
hero. Asked if he thought football was a life-and-death
matter, he had once famously replied, 'No, it's much more
important than that!'

Over the next three years I played many times with the
Liverpool reserve side though, much to my regret, I never
made the first team. However, I did meet, train and socialise
with many of the star players. The first-team fullback Gerry
Byrne and I had lots of laughs together.

One laugh we shared was when some prankster had
removed all the toilet rolls from the dressing-room toilets.
The latest Bill Shankly signing, Tony Hateley, was the butt
of this joke. I was sitting in the dressing room with Gerry
Byrne and we saw Tony minus his lower garments run in
from the toilets, open his locker and remove his new silver-
grey mohair jacket. Clutching this, he retreated, throwing us
a look that could curdle milk.

Later, in the canteen, we were drinking tea with Roy
Evans, who was an up-and-coming first-team player at the
time. Gerry Byrne was telling Roy that he had just seen the
strangest thing, Tony Hateley taking his new jacket into the
toilets. At the next table Jimmy Bowman and Lee Koo, two
other players, started laughing. 'We have to see this!' said
Jimmy and set off running to the dressing rooms. Unable to
resist seeing what this was about, we followed.

The scene we came across in the toilets was quite sad
really. Tony Hateley had been caught short and, in desperation, had ripped up the lining of his mohair jacket. Jimmy

Bowman was rolling about laughing, as he had obviously been responsible for this practical joke.

As I watched Jimmy enjoying himself at the expense of Tony, who had been lording it over the rest of the team, a spirit appeared. At the time I very rarely saw such things, so this was quite a shock to me. But I clearly saw this discarnate being; he was an old man, looked to be in his late seventies, and he stood next to Jimmy Bowman. 'Tell Jimmy this man has more to learn.' The spirit pointed at Tony. 'You and Jimmy will be in Ireland,' the spirit told me, and vanished.

I was thunderstruck for a moment. When I described the man I had just seen to Jimmy, he said that the description fitted his late grandfather exactly.

The remark about Tony was true. The man had a rather unfortunate way of assuming he was more important than the other team members. Eventually Tony moved on from Liverpool FC and out of football altogether. As for the spirit's prediction about Ireland, well, that came true too.

In 1968 I was playing a five-a-side training match with the first team. I can still remember who was there: Roy Evans, Joe Fagan, Ronnie Moran, Ian Callaghan, Reuben Bennett, Stuart Mason, Chris Lawler, Peter Hall and Allen Hughes. The game was a bit rough and tumble and suddenly Ronnie Moran brought Allen Hughes down with a tackle. Instantly they were at each other's throats.

As I stood and watched these two team colleagues hurling insults and abuse at each other, I became aware that Allen Hughes was about to leave Liverpool. I know he loved playing for the Reds but his time at Anfield was almost over. I could see a vision of him walking away from the ground and knew he would never return.

Shortly afterwards Bill Shankly sold Allen Hughes to Chester City FC.

I sometimes confided my visions to other players and often they would ask me to give them my thoughts on their careers. I couldn't quite do that then. I was not actively seeking to be a medium for the spirit world and was far from developed as any kind of effective channel. But the spirit world did not give up on me. Every now and then they would pop a message or a vision through. I just accepted the gifts I had, but others thought me very odd indeed.

Some months after Allen Hughes moved to Chester City FC I played his team in a pre-season friendly. I asked him how he was settling in and we had a friendly chat. Then, much to my astonishment, I saw a huge chicken leg beside Allen Hughes and the trade name 'Kentucky Fried' came into my mind. So I told Allen exactly what I had seen. 'You, my mate, are one weird person,' he replied, and that was that.

Some years later I was at a wedding reception in Liverpool city centre when I met Allen Hughes again. 'Ah! The chicken-leg kid!' he said, jogging my memory. 'You know something, Derek,' he went on. 'Just after we played that friendly in '68, I left Chester and went to work as an area manager for Kentucky Fried!'

Naturally, Allen wanted to know if there was anything else I could see for him in the future. But at the time I could not communicate to order with the spirit world; visions came to me without warning or didn't come at all. However, I did not want to disappoint Allen too much so I told him that his life was going to be a happy one. If he believed that, then he was halfway there already. Self-belief is at least 50 per cent of any success story.

After training, many of the players would often go for a cup of coffee to the Kardomah Café in Bold Street. It was the place to be seen in the late 1960s and lots of the Merseybeat bands called in to mix with the Everton and Liverpool football players who frequented this café. One afternoon I was in the Kardomah with Emlyn Hughes, Peter Wall and Stuart Mason talking about the practice match we had just played. As we spoke, I saw a vision of a crushed car with Emlyn standing next to it.

'Do you have a car?' I asked him. I had never seen him driving one.

'Not right at the moment,' Emlyn replied, 'but I'm getting a brand-new one tomorrow.'

I told him of my vision, but he was sure nothing was going to happen to him.

The next day the team was training at Melwood and I noticed that Emlyn Hughes wasn't present. I asked Peter Wall where he was. 'Oh, don't worry, he'll be here soon,' he said. We were just running out to form sides for a game when I heard someone calling to the coach, Reuben Bennett, from the touch line, 'Emlyn's going to be late. He's fine, but his new car's a write-off.'

When Emlyn arrived, he ran straight over to me. 'How did you know?'

Well, I couldn't at that time explain, I just knew. No wonder many of the Liverpool players thought I was weird – I was beginning to think so myself.

Time passed at Anfield and eventually it became clear that I was not going to make it into the first team at Liverpool FC. Bill Shankly had always been positive about my abilities but when he called me into his office just before my eighteenth birthday, I knew it was to close my career with his club. There were, he said, many teams that wanted to sign me as a full-time first-team professional, but my Liverpool days were over.

I was very upset about this. I had dreamed for so long of wearing the famous Liverpool FC red shirt and running out onto the turf at Anfield, their home ground, playing for the best team in the world. Bill Shankly's Liverpool side of the mid- to late 1960s was a major force in European football. Sadly, I was no longer to be a part of it.

As I walked to the bus stop, carrying my kit in my now far from new duffel bag, I thought of that happy day when I had scored for Bootle Boys and met Bill Shankly. The bus was late, it rained, and I was just so disappointed. Standing there, getting wetter and wetter, I remembered the words of the spirit guide. 'We are with you,' he had said. 'You'll never walk alone.' So, as the bus still hadn't arrived, we set off walking to the next stop. And it rained.

PLAYING PROFESSIONAL FOOTBALL

My new football club was Wrexham FC, the team that had originally signed me when I was thirteen. The manager was called Arfon Williams and I got along well with both him and the other players. However, halfway through my first season with Wrexham, Arfon Williams was sacked. He called me into his office and told me he was leaving. As he spoke, I sensed a terrible darkness around him. I knew something awful lay immediately before him but the details were not disclosed to me.

A few months later, as my first and only season with Wrexham was coming to an end, I saw headlines in a national newspaper that sickened me deeply. Arfon Williams had been charged with murder. Later he was found guilty of shooting a man and sent to prison. My vision of the darkness that was before him came flooding back to me. I might have been a professional football player now, but my hidden powers still surfaced from time to time.

The reason I left Wrexham was a better offer from the Northern Irish side Glentoran, and also to join up with Alex Young, known as the Golden Vision, a player I knew and respected.

As I sat in the airport departure lounge waiting to fly to Belfast, I saw a football player called Tommy Jackson. He knew about me from my days at Liverpool and came over to say he was off to join Everton, my father's favourite team. As he spoke, I saw an image of him walking away from Goodison Park, Everton's home ground. In this vision I saw standing behind him the smiling face of the top Everton star player of the day, Alan Ball.

Within just a few months of joining Everton, Tommy Jackson was transferred out. The sports pages of the national press carried stories of his arguments with the player Alan Ball. 'Big Bust-Up at Everton' the headlines said, alongside a picture of Alan Ball, who was smiling.

The Glentoran team went to play in the South of Ireland. Who should come running out for the opposing side but Jimmy Bowman? 'Check the loo for toilet rolls, lads!' I shouted, as we lined up for the kick off. 'Jimmy likes to hide them!' After the match we met and had a bit of a chuckle about that incident at Liverpool FC. We also talked about the problems Jimmy's victim Tony Hateley had recently been facing. 'Just like you predicted,' Jimmy said. But in a way he was wrong. It was the spirit of his grandfather who had predicted that; I was just the medium.

At the end of just one season I left Glentoran FC when Alex Young did, and for a while played full-time for Stockport County FC. I was not really making a brilliant success of my career as a football player. But around this time, at my sister's engagement party, I met a seventeen-year-old girl called Joan. She was a lovely, sensitive lady. Within a year, we had married; I was all of twenty-two.

The year 1972 was a wonderful year. My wife gave birth to a beautiful baby boy we named Carl. But my ambitions as a professional football player were unfulfilled. I knew – well, I thought I knew – that with the right team I could be a big success. So when the secretary of the players' union based in Manchester asked me if I was in any way interested in playing for a foreign side, I said yes.

Within a few weeks I had signed on the dotted line and was flying out to Australia. Which is on the other side of the world from Liverpool, as Joan kept pointing out.

ANTIPODEAN ADVENTURES

I had signed a contract to play for a club called USC Lion in the South Australian League. The club officials and the players were really nice to us, and found us a respectable house in a decent neighbourhood. The sun shone and it shone some more, then it was sunny and, well, it wasn't Liverpool. However, my wife could not bear to be away from her home town. She missed all her friends and family. No matter how hard I tried, Joan would not settle in Australia.

I attempted to get her interested in the local culture. I myself was very keen to learn all I could about the Australian Aboriginal tribes. The secretary of my football club, Vladimir Potesni, was also the assistant curator of the local history museum in Adelaide. There were ancient artefacts in the vaults of the museum that were not for public display. Vladimir kindly let me see these and taught me about them. There were such things as boomerangs dating back thousands of years and stones inscribed with magical symbols. To me that museum was a wonderland and I learned so much. Vladimir also introduced me to the occupants of an Aboriginal settlement in the Barossa valley. Here I met an elder of the tribe known only as Jacko. He and I became great friends.

Jacko was a very wise old Australian Aborigine; he knew many things about the nature of the landscape in which he had been raised. Jacko would spend hours telling me of the strange rituals that he and his fellow tribesmen practised. They believed in the power of nature linked to the spirit world where their ancestors lived. To Jacko and his people, death held no fear, indeed they accepted it as just another stage of life. 'You can be like me, Derek,' Jacko would often say; 'one day you will be.' By which he meant that I had psychic powers within me. Jacko was, in his way, telling me that I should accept my path and become a medium for the spirit world. The time was approaching when I would heed his advice.

One day Jacko took me to meet a nephew of his called Davey. Now Davey was a hunter who had mastered the art of throwing boomerangs. Anyone who has ever tried to get a boomerang to come back will recognise that this is very difficult indeed. There are, Davey told me, four different types of boomerang and each has its own peculiarities. The one Davey used for killing prey, such as kangaroos, was quite small. It was not much larger than the palm of a man's hand.

Davey showed me how to throw it. I chucked the thing all over the place, practising, but my boomerang wouldn't come back.

Out in the Australian bush with Jacko and Davey I felt a peace that I had never known before. 'You are awakening,' Jacko said to me many, many times. Strange dreams came to me at night during my close association with those wonderful tribesmen. I would see myself standing in the open bush surrounded by people that I somehow seemed to know, yet I didn't. Flashes of inspiration and visions of the future came to me more often now. I'm quite certain that being close to Jacko helped to open my psychic channels and prepare me to be that which I was destined to become.

One day Jacko brought me into the tribal encampment and took me into his dwelling. There he showed me a tray full of stones set into metal. One item on this tray was a huge silver ring that Jacko insisted I place on my finger. It fitted me perfectly. 'That ring is for you,' Jacko said. 'It is a friendship ring and when you leave Australia, it will bring you back.' Then that big guy took my hand and held it very gently in his. For a brief moment I seemed to see his thoughts and a feeling of peace came over me.

I still have that ring and treasure it deeply. Whenever I see it, I think of those distant days in the Australian bush with my friend Jacko. He passed away to the spirit world many years ago, but he isn't dead. He lives on in the world beyond, happy with his tribesmen. Sometimes in my dreams I see him still. We are standing out in the sun-beaten bush surrounded by others that I somehow know, but yet I don't.

My career as a player with USC Lion was going fine. I was voted Player of the Year and was even selected to represent Southern Australia. I flourished in that glorious sunshine and was playing the best football of my life. I even turned out against British teams touring Australia and met many players I had known in England. It was a great adventure and one I shall never forget.

It was in Australia that I gave my first private psychic readings to individuals and even groups. I had given the odd message to my team mates, telling them what I had 'seen' for them – things like house moves and children being born. Sometimes I got visions of transfers to other teams and I was usually right. Soon the word got around the football clubs that I was psychic and the wives of the players often asked me to give them a reading. It was not my best work, I realise that now, but I was certainly beginning to awaken spiritually at this time.

One specific incident from those early days stays in my mind and is a warning to anyone who has visions of disasters. I had previously given a psychic reading to a lady in Adelaide called Debbie. She worked in a factory producing optical lenses. One afternoon, during a quiet period, I suddenly saw a vision of Debbie surrounded by flames.

As quickly as I could, I contacted her husband by telephone and told him I saw that his wife was in danger. At first he thought I was joking but my tone obviously convinced him that I wasn't. He said that Debbie had already left home for work and was on the late-afternoon shift.

In my mind I knew I had to get to this factory and save Debbie from what I was quite certain was an impending fire or explosion. When I arrived at the factory gates in my car, I didn't know what to say. So I just asked if I could possibly speak to Debbie on a matter of some urgency. The security guard at the gate took some persuading, but eventually Debbie was brought out from the factory to see me. I soon convinced her that my vision of fire was related to her and for safety she should go directly home. She did.

On my way back to my own house I realised that I had left behind a factory full of people that I sensed were in danger. I just couldn't leave them to their fate so I turned my car round and went back to the security guard at the factory gates. At first he thought I was just a crank and told me to get off before he called the police. But when he realised I was serious, he took action. The fire brigade arrived, emergency

services were called out and I, well, I was taken to Adelaide
Police Station and locked in a cell.

Hours passed and I was really weary from the constant
questioning. They thought I had planted a bomb or was an
arsonist, a terrorist, some such thing. When I spoke of my
clairvoyance, one senior detective said to me, 'You say you're
a witch?' I was not getting very far trying to explain that I
had psychic powers and could see visions of the future. All I
could see then was visions of myself inside secure accommo-
dation. Those Australian police officers were definitely not
amused to hear that my gran was a medium and could talk to
spirits. I had had the entire Adelaide emergency service
teams chasing round a factory I said was threatened by fire
and they had found nothing.

The police eventually let me go. The next day at USC
Lion, I got called everything from 'Joan of Sparks' to 'the
Calamity Kid'. They all had a good laugh.

That weekend the factory burned to the ground.
Thankfully there had been no one in the place as it was
closed. When the fire service report came in, it showed that
there had been an electrical short-circuit that had ignited
chemicals used within the processing unit. The place had
gone up like a rocket.

So I was proved correct, but not before I had suffered a
great deal of humiliation. Would I do it again? Well, I would
not need to now that I am a developed medium and can seek
clarification from my spirit guide. But then I was just awakening.

One clairvoyant episode at that time concerned myself. I was
in a TV rental shop in Adelaide looking at the latest television sets and thinking about hiring one. The store had
numerous sets of varying make, size and manufacture on
display. They were all switched on and tuned to the same
channel so that the customers could select the picture they
liked best. However, as I looked at these sets I saw that one
was tuned to a different station from the rest.

As I watched the programme playing on this set, I saw a plane on a runway with a long queue of people boarding it. Imagine my surprise as I saw my wife Joan, holding our baby Carl, and myself stood in the queue. 'Look at that!' I shouted to the shop owner, who turned and stared at the set I was pointing to. As I watched I saw my family and myself enter the plane. 'That's me!' I said. 'Look, I'm on TV!' But the owner just stared at me as though I were insane. When I looked again, the picture had changed and the set was tuned to the same channel as the rest of them. I knew then that it was a sign from the world beyond that soon we would return to England.

And so it was to be. Within a month of my seeing that vision in the TV rental shop, we were on our way back to Liverpool. Joan was happy but I, once more freezing in the rain, was not. Worse, my football days were behind me. I left them with the sunshine at USC Lion. For a while I played part-time with Marine AFC, but I had to find a new way to make a living. For the first time in my life I was looking for what people call a job. The prospect scared me. I was approaching thirty and all I knew was football.

WORKING FOR A LIVING

For a time I worked at a big factory owned by the Courtaulds company. My job was in the cotton-spinning rooms. My fellow workers were great fun, and for the first time in my life I felt relaxed at my place of employment. There was no competition at Courtaulds, you simply did your job and drew your pay at the end of the week. There is a lot to be said for working in a factory.

After about six months, rumours started that the factory was about to close. This caused me to worry so much that I could hardly sleep. Things had been going so well, I enjoyed that work and it gave us the regular money we needed to rent a house. Now everything was going to be turned upside down.

During the early hours of one sleepless night I received a visit from the spirit world. I heard a voice in my mind saying to me, 'Do not worry, son. This is your time.' I knew that voice and looked up to see standing at the foot of my bed the materialised form of my gran. She was smiling at me and looked just as she had all those years before when she had held me close and told me I was special.

That was it! I was special, I was a medium and I had been visited by my gran to tell me that this was the time to use my gifts. Now I really couldn't sleep, not because I was worried but because I was so excited. A plan formed in my mind. I would use my ability to communicate with the spirit world to earn a living. I would charge people for the service that I had previously given freely.

I jumped out of bed, ran downstairs and began to write out a small advertisement to put in the local paper: 'Derek Acorah: Clairvoyant Medium. Personal readings at home £2.50 per person.' Many people knew me in the area and everyone who was interested in psychic matters knew of my gran. So as soon as the clock struck nine I telephoned the Bootle press and placed my advertisement. Within days of its appearing in the papers, I was fully booked for weeks. And I have been busy ever since.

In my private work I never used any props, such as a crystal ball or Tarot cards. I had no use for such things, although there were many people who remarked on their absence. I just tuned myself in to the vibrations surrounding the client and asked my spirit guide Sam for help. This was all I required and it is all any true medium requires. To me the crystals and cards are just props like those used by a magician on stage, and I'm not into hocus pocus.

The job at Courtaulds did end in redundancy and I was now earning my living as a full-time professional medium. Frequently this required me to be out late at night visiting groups, mainly female groups, in their homes. I remember going to one house in Albert Schweitzer Avenue, Sefton, to see a group of ladies. I arrived at 10.30 a.m. and knocked on the door. A huge lady with curlers in her hair and a cigarette smouldering in her mouth opened the door. 'Yeh?' she said, looking at me as though I was a door-to-door brush sales-man. 'Wor is it?' I told her I was Derek, the medium that they had booked. 'You him then?' she said and motioned me to enter. Such enthusiasm, I thought.

Inside the house I was taken into the front lounge where an old lady was sitting. She stared at me with steely eyes. 'Go on then,' she said, 'what can you see?' This was rather offputting, but as I looked at this stern figure sitting before me, I became aware of a coffin with a man's body in it. I was drawn towards the left wrist and saw that it bore the signs of a watch strap, but there was no watch. Then I heard the voice of the spirit of this body speaking to me quite clearly: 'Tell her she shouldn't have given my watch away.' I passed this information to the lady, who very nearly fell off her chair.

'Go on then,' she said, straightening herself, 'what else is there?'

I listened as the spirit spoke again: 'Tell my wife if she doesn't put my watch back in my coffin, I'll be round again tonight!'

When I told her that, she jumped up and ran out of the room, shouting, 'I told you it was him!' She had woken the night before in the early hours to find her bedroom full of a white, luminous mist. This had scared her quite a bit as her husband had just passed away and she thought it was his ghost returning. She was right. He had come for his gold watch.

'I gave it to our Tommy,' she said, 'but I better get it back. I don't want him coming round haunting me!'

After passing on that message, I was inundated with requests for private readings in the Albert Schweitzer Road area.

As word got around that I was the real thing, my workload increased. Sometimes I would see fifteen people a day for private readings. This was far too much, but I loved my work. Over the next few years I must have seen over 25,000 individuals as a professional medium. I was able to buy a nice new home close to where my parents lived in Bootle. My son Carl was settled into school and everything was going smoothly – too smoothly. I had been paying far more attention to my work than to my wife.

One morning in 1982 I woke up and realised that my marriage was over. Joan and I had been growing gradually apart over the last three to four years and, while I still deeply respected her, I knew our days together were at an end. There was no traumatic ending to our relationship, no hurtful scenes, just the sad recognition that we were now two people with very different lives to live. The parting was amicable. Carl had our decision explained to him and he was old enough to understand. There were no tears, just a rather empty goodbye as I closed the door on the girl I had once loved more than anything in the whole world.

Joan's second husband would be a joiner, I told her – and so it turned out to be.

After the break-up of my marriage I moved into a house on my own and began to see people in the main lounge for private readings. That was a big mistake. For some reason many people thought it OK to use my carpets and furniture as an ashtray. Within a few months there were cigarette burns all over the settee, and people had stamped their cigarette butts into the carpet. All I needed was a dartboard and my lounge might as well have been a pub. I soon stopped that.

For a while I had a shop which I converted to use as an office and waiting room. This worked quite well for a while but I was not doing my best work at the time. I was lonely and needed to find some peace of mind. My divorce papers had been processed and finalised. There was nothing to drive me on, no one to need me. So I locked up my shop, got into my car and drove non-stop to the port of Plymouth. I just had to get away.

In Plymouth I stayed at a nice hotel and was relaxing over

a glass of wine in the cabaret lounge listening to the resident female singer. She was pretty good, I thought. So at the interval, between her two spots, I went over and bought her a drink. She accepted and suggested we meet for a talk when her work was over. At the end of a rousing 'My, my, my Delilah!' this lady joined me and we got along really well. There was something about her that touched something inside me. Then I realised what it was. She was psychic!

When I told her this, she quickly agreed and said her mother had been a medium for many years. Then she gave me a remarkable message: 'You are going back to Liverpool. There you will meet a woman called Gwen. She has an infirm mother who can't walk. You'll marry Gwen.'

Within two months of returning to Liverpool from my escape break at Plymouth, I was invited to a party where I was introduced to a lady by the name of Gwen. We instantly recognised each other as like-minded souls and have been together ever since. Indeed, we are now married and care for Gwen's aged mother, who is very infirm and cannot walk.

It was a rather blustery afternoon in late September and Gwen suggested we have a day out at Blackpool, the seaside town noted for fresh air and fun. There was certainly plenty of fresh air, together with buckets of rain. After walking ten yards along the promenade, we gave up. Clutching our sodden fish and chips, we climbed back into the car and headed towards home. An overturned lorry blocked the road out of Blackpool so we took a diversion through the ancient city of Lancaster.

As we drove through the still pouring rain, I saw a sign near Lancaster city centre. 'Spiritualist Church' it said and indicated a turning on my immediate left. It can only have been guidance from the world beyond that made me drive into this street and enter the church. I had been an occasional visitor to Spiritualist churches all my life but had not been planning to visit one that day.

Inside the church there was a medium on the platform

talking to the congregation and giving messages. There were perhaps fifty people present and many of them did receive messages. Suddenly the lady on the platform pointed towards the back of the church, where I was sitting, and said, 'Derek, I have a message for you from the Boss.'

I was a bit taken aback by this. Was she talking to me? I didn't know anybody called 'the Boss'. So I kept silent.

The medium, Gloria Duthie, was having none of that. 'Right, Derek, I know you're there. The Boss says you're going to score more goals in your work now than you ever did at Liverpool.'

'I'm Derek!' I called and stood up so Gloria Duthie could see me.

'Well, Derek, this man says he was your boss and you know him. He's a Scottish man and has grey hair.' It had to be Bill Shankly. The boss of Liverpool FC had passed to spirit some years before and I had shed tears at hearing the sad news. I respected and, in a funny way, loved that tough old guy. He was my hero.

'Derek,' said Gloria, 'will you come up here and take this service? You can, you know. You are a very special man.'

The following week I did just that. I went back to Lancaster Spiritualist church and gave my first public demonstration of platform mediumship. My gran would have been so proud! She said I had a special gift and now I was really going to use it for the benefit of all those who cared to listen.

Since that day I have been on public platforms all around the UK and in many foreign countries. But, no matter where I go or what I achieve, I will never forget what my gran taught me as a child. 'Tell the truth and give only that which you receive from the world of spirit,' she said. I have, I always will, and in doing so I hope that those in need of proof that life is eternal will find it in my words. For my words come from the world beyond, where truth and the love of God are as one.

Messages of Hope

In the many years I have been a professional medium, there have been times when the individual seeking advice through my mediumship has been in despair. Let me stress that this is not the general rule. Most people visit me to seek a connection with a lost loved one, or just out of curiosity. But there are those for whom life has reached a crisis point. Here are a few examples of messages that brought hope to people in need – I am one of them.

MARRIED TO A MONSTER

I frequently see people who are in the grip of some family crisis that they can't quite cope with. Often there is a simple solution but they are avoiding making the moves that have to be made to resolve the matter. In June 1994 a lady came to see me with just such a problem. Deep inside she knew what she had to do but she wanted help to make the decision to do it. She sought that help from me through my mediumship.

As this lady sat with me in my office, I saw not the weary, worn-out figure of someone whose life has been full of hardship, but a beautiful young girl. I saw this middle-aged lady as she had been over twenty years ago. I knew that this poor woman had suffered terribly, through the agency of another.

As I looked at her, I could sense the spirit of her grandfather. He had been a dockyard worker in Liverpool and stood by the side of his granddaughter now, bringing her the strength she would soon require. When I described this man to her and gave her the name of Billy, she cried. I heard this tough but very gentle man speak to me in my mind. 'Tell our Jean to divorce that brute,' he said. 'Tell her I've seen him beating her.' When I passed this information to her, this dear lady sobbed and said, 'Derek, what can I do?'

I make no claims to be a counsellor and only give that which I receive from the spirit world, so I simply told this lady to do as the spirit of her grandfather said.

'But he will kill me!' she said. Then she told me a terrible tale of abuse and injury. I nearly wept myself as the anguish of the lady overcame me.

Looking to her side, I saw now the spirit of this poor woman's grandmother. 'I'm Sarah, her granny,' she said. She was only small but dressed so neatly in a black dress with a white blouse and there was a very determined look on her face. 'Tell her to get the police on him! He's a monster, not a man,' the spirit of Sarah said. So I did, and told the lady who had spoken. She wiped her eyes and looked up at me. 'I will, Derek, I will,' she said.

Before this lady left my office, I handed her an audio-cassette recording of the messages I had passed. Many more of her friends and relatives alive in the world beyond had visited to give her hope and confirmation that she was right to do as her grandmother Sarah had said. Shaking her hand, I wished her well and watched as she walked away from my office. There was a spring to her step now and I knew she would soon be free from her beast of a husband.

In September of the same year, a man I had never seen before had booked the last session of the day. There was nothing unusual in that, though perhaps 80 per cent of my clients are female. However, I invited this man in and sat him down in the chair directly opposite me, preparing to give of my mediumship. He was a huge man, powerfully built and over six foot tall. He seemed very ill at ease and I tried to relax him by suggesting he remove his overcoat and perhaps smoke a cigarette.

'Do you know who I am?' he asked me in a very threatening voice. Then he pulled from his pocket an audio cassette. 'A monster, am I?' he shouted.

Before I could move, this brute had me by the throat and was dragging me towards the window. I struggled but he was too strong for me. With just one hand he held me against the wall and with the other he opened the window.

'Beast, am I?' he yelled.

I was fast becoming faint and he had forced my upper body out of the window. Looking down, I could see the heads of people walking along Victoria Street, three floors below.

Suddenly the door burst open and the security guard ran in with two of the secretaries from the offices next door to mine. They grabbed my assailant and fought him to the floor. Gasping for breath, I fell forwards onto my desk, lifted the telephone and dialled the emergency number for the police. They came and arrested this crazy man.

Of course, he was the husband of the lady who had been to see me in June. She had taken the advice of her grandmother's spirit and reported him to the police. Unfortunately for me, this poor woman had told someone that it was I who had given her this message of hope, and they had told her husband. When he got bail from police custody, he had set out to seek revenge.

The last I heard, he was serving a long prison sentence for violent offences he had committed in Liverpool where he worked as a club bouncer. He had very nearly thrown me out of my office window, thirty feet up, and I don't think that I would have bounced. You meet all kinds in this work.

THE MISSING CHILDREN

It had been a busy morning in my Liverpool office and I was sitting quietly enjoying a cup of coffee and some biscuits between seeing clients. As I dunked the third chocolate digestive into my cup, the door opened and a group of ladies walked in. There was a look of grim determination on the face of the one who spoke. 'Derek, you have to help us! Our children are missing.'

There were five ladies and between them they told me that three of their children had gone missing the day before and could not be found. The police had searched everywhere and, they said, seemed unable to do more. The fear in the voices of those poor mothers hurt me. I was almost overcome with emotion myself as I felt the anguish in their troubled minds. I could see their tear-stained faces looking at me and I knew that they considered me to be their final hope.

I had to do something, but what? I had never tried to find a missing person before. For a second or two I closed my eyes and asked my spirit guide Sam to help me.

'It's his Liverpool supporter's scarf,' one lady said, handing me her son's red and white woollen scarf. I took it from her but had no idea what I was going to get from it. Suddenly I saw a vision of a garage with a green-painted door. I knew the children were behind this door. 'Give me more, Sam!' I said in my mind. 'Please, Sam, give me more.'

The vision changed and I saw a tall, thin man with unkempt hair. I knew he was responsible for taking these children. I also sensed he was not from Liverpool and spoke with a distinct accent.

Before me the group of ladies were waiting anxiously. 'Sam, more . . . give me more, please.' I said in my mind.

Then I saw another vision; it was a road sign. 'Davenport Road' it said. I knew then that the youngsters would be found safe and the man who had abducted them would be arrested as he went back to molest the children. But the police had to act quickly, before this man returned to his victims.

I gave the ladies the information I had seen in my visions and told them to act immediately. Their children were in desperate danger.

All five mothers ran out of my office and over the road to the police station there. I had done all I could and said a quiet prayer of thanks to God and to my guide.

I had just returned to my soggy biscuit when the office door opened and in stamped six foot something of angry uniform. It was a police sergeant and he did not look happy. 'I could arrest you under the Witchcraft Act!' he said, poking me in the chest with his radio. 'You leave the policing to the police or you'll find yourself in the cells!'

Knowing they hadn't burned any witches in England since the 1600s, I felt pretty safe.

'Who told you to tell those women that load of nonsense?' the sergeant went on.

For a moment I considered trying to explain to the man that I had received the information from my spirit guide Sam. But I thought better of it. 'It's true!' I ventured. 'You will find those children inside a garage with a green door on Davenport Road.'

The sergeant's face went three shades of crimson. 'If I hear one more word from you, buster . . .!' He about-turned and marched off to arrest some hapless motorists.

Back at the police station, those desperate mothers demanded to see the detective inspector in charge of the case. He listened carefully to what I had told them and, unlike the blue giant, he decided to pay attention. After all, what other hope did they have?

When the police went to Davenport Road, they found a row of locked garages. One of these had a green door and when they forced it open they found inside the three missing children. Then, just as I had seen in my vision, a tall, thin man returned to the garage and was arrested by the police. He was from out of town, had unkempt hair and spoke with a thick Geordie accent.

The following day the five ladies came to thank me for helping them in their hour of need. With them came the detective inspector who had been thoughtful enough to act on my information. 'You are a remarkable man, Derek,' he said and shook my hand. I was sorry he hadn't brought the sergeant along.

THE GHOST OF RADIO CITY

My career as a professional psychic medium was certainly paying me a living wage, but somehow I felt that there was more I could do. Many mediums want to take their gift and present it to the public on the stage or through the media. I too wanted to do this, but how?

I always trust in my spirit guide Sam. During meditation he had said that there was to be a major new development for me. That message gave me great hope, and I was excited at the prospect of a new challenge. Mediums rarely receive messages for themselves, just lots of encouragement and help from the spirit world. I do on occasion see flashes or visions of forthcoming events that involve myself, but mostly I 'see' for other people.

I was delighted to be invited by the radio host Kev Seed of the Liverpool City radio station Radio City to appear on his morning show in 1998. I sat in the studio taking calls from the public and tuning in to the world beyond for them. The calls were coming in from all over Merseyside and Kev seemed really pleased with the way it was going. The subjects were very varied. There were ladies phoning in wanting advice on domestic matters. There were also men who were totally sceptical, for a while at least. It was great fun and I was enjoying myself when I looked up to see a discarnate entity standing in the doorway.

Kev was obviously totally unaware that we had a ghostly visitor. This spirit smiled at me, turned and walked out through the closed studio door.

During the commercial break I asked Kev if he knew that Radio City was haunted. His response surprised me. He ran out into the reception area to call for one of the station's senior staff. Soon the regional director, John Myers, joined us in the studio. John is a huge man, six foot four and built like Arnold Schwarzenegger's big brother. Kev put a record on and then, off the air, he told John that I had seen 'the ghost'.

It seemed that the late-night talk-show host Pete Price had been halfway through a show one evening the previous week when he had felt a hand on his shoulder. Knowing that he was in the studio alone, Pete was startled. Looking up, he had seen a semi-transparent ghostly figure walking through the closed studio door. Just as I had, in the very same studio.

John Myers asked me to describe the spirit I had seen. Late middle age, about five foot six, dressed in casual clothes. I got the impression that this ghost had worked at the station as a kind of general assistant. He had returned because he loved being at Radio City. He probably enjoyed the mixture of anarchic humour and music that this Liverpool radio station is rightly famous for.

John Myers just laughed at this. 'Oh, really?' he said.

Even as he spoke, I heard the voice of the spirit addressing me. 'People don't believe you, but they will next Monday because at 9 a.m. precisely I will spin the hands of this studio clock backwards.' So I told Kev and John.

They seemed quite amused by this. 'Tell the listeners, Derek,' Kev said, 'then on Monday I'll watch that clock and we'll see if your ghost is telling the truth.' So – and this is a matter of public record – I went back on air and told the Radio City listeners that the ghost of this radio station would spin the studio clock hands backwards at 9 a.m. next Monday morning. In the background I could hear the repressed chuckling of the massive Mr Myers.

On the next Monday morning I went into my office in Liverpool an hour early. I wanted to listen to Kev Seed's show and see if my friend the ghost would keep his promise to me. I switched on the portable radio I had brought with me. 'Twenty-five minutes to go to the ghost's deadline,' Kev Seed said on air. He sounded quite light-hearted, as though this was a great giggle. Then he played some music.

'Three minutes to go!' Kev said. 'The studio is full, we even have John Myers standing under the clock. Is there anybody there?' And so it went until Kev Seed began the countdown to 9 a.m. 'Ten . . . nine . . . eight . . . seven . . . six . . . five . . . four . . . three . . . two . . . My God!'

The hands of the clock had begun to spin backwards.

That ghost had proved a point, to Kev Seed and Mr Myers at least. I was invited back the very next day and I've been the resident psychic medium there ever since. I still see that ghostly clock-stopper from time to time. He gives me a friendly wave and I always acknowledge him. After all, he did me a very big favour; he got me my favourite job in the world – talking to the wonderful Liverpool people on Radio City.

PENNIES FROM HEAVEN

One morning not long afterwards I was driving from my home in Southport to Radio City in the centre of Liverpool to broadcast my regular weekly slot on a phone-in and music programme called *The Billy and Wally Show*. (It has since become the *The Billy Butler Show*.) The freezing mists of this December day had caught the motorists by surprise and the roads were congested. So I turned off my usually route and onto the B5193.

On Seaforth Road in Litherland I stopped to buy a packet of cigarettes. Some day I will give up this habit. As I stepped out of the shop, I saw a weary-looking man leaning against the shop's entrance. He was around thirty years old, about my height, wearing what looked like a rather wet overcoat. There was an air of despair about him that instantly touched me. 'Got any change, mate?' he asked. Reaching into my pocket, I pulled out what little change I had, about 60p, and passed it to him. As our hands touched, I noticed he was freezing cold. Sensing his desperation, I offered him half my packet of cigarettes.

'My wife threw me out last night,' the man told me. 'I lost my job, got made redundant, I didn't dare tell her as we have three children and Christmas is coming. Then she found out from a friend and threw me out. She said I was useless.'

For a moment his hopelessness became mine. Being psychic, I am sometimes swamped by another person's emotions. Suddenly I was cold, I felt wet, weary and there was nothing to live for. But I can draw back from those feelings; this poor man couldn't. Taking a deep breath, I asked my spirit guide Sam if he could help.

At once the answer came to me and I knew that he would be home with his family long before Christmas. Although it must have sounded strange, I told the man that I was a spirit medium and that I had a message of hope for him. I could see that he only partly believed me, but he thanked me just the same and shook my hand.

As I started to walk back towards my car, I saw something on the pavement by my right shoe. Reaching down, I picked up what looked to me like a neatly folded piece of paper. It was a bank note and I knew it was intended for the man to whom I had been speaking. 'This is for you,' I said, unfolding that ten-pound note and placing it in his hand. 'Take this as proof that you are being helped from the world of spirit and have no need to fear.'

There were tears in the man's eyes as he thanked me. Yet it was not I who had brought hope to him; that came through me from the world beyond. There are times when even I am amazed.

THE AMERICAN SOLUTION

A man called Taffy Jones came to my office in September 1988. His financial circumstances had become desperate and he dared not even discuss them with his wife. In search of an answer Taffy had come to me.

People talk about a black cloud of depression; as a psychic, I can see this around individuals trapped by their own anguish. Taffy was surrounded with an aura of dark grey and was clearly edging towards the point when his final reserve would give out. Any moment he was expecting to find himself bankrupt. When he asked for my help, this man meant it.

Looking into Taffy's eyes I saw a decent man who had lost his way in this cruel material world. As I opened my psychic channels, searching for an answer to Taffy's plight, I saw a vision of another man. This man was not Taffy, though he looked very much like him. Then I heard a voice speaking to me: 'By tonight the problem will be solved.'

You can imagine how hard it was telling a desperate man that, but I did. 'Go home and telephone me tonight because the answer will be at your home this very evening.'

Taffy looked at me in utter disbelief. 'Is that it?' he said. It was.

The day's work over, I drove home to walk the dogs and watch TV with Gwen. Taffy was in my mind but he didn't call me until the following day.

'My brother in America, he's telephoned me to say he's just won a fortune on the lottery! He wants me to fly to America, he's sending me a ticket!'

Taffy not only cleared his debts, but his brother gave him enough money to buy his wife the beautiful big house she had always dreamed of. Years later Taffy Jones came into my Liverpool office to thank me. He is now prosperous and happy.

PLUMBING THE HEIGHTS

In the late 1980s, a man called George Hindley came to me for a private reading. I sensed that I had a sceptic before me, but he was obviously willing to listen or he would not have been at my office. George told me his sister had persuaded him to come along. I've noticed that many men seem to need to explain to me that they are attending under protest.

As George spoke, I knew he was really fed up with his job. He'd been apprenticed as a plumber on leaving school and now, in his mid-thirties, he was still plumbing. He wanted to do something more with his life and I could see very clearly that a new pathway was about to open before him.

'You're going to own a wine bar on Standish Street in Anfield,' I said. In my mind I could see George running this business and it was going to be very successful.

A look of incredulity appeared on his face. 'You have to be joking, mate!' He nearly fell off his chair laughing. 'I'm a plumber, not a snooty wine-bar type!'

But I knew he was wrong. 'Then you buy a cabaret club and this is even more successful,' I told him.

'Wait till I tell my missus what your predictions are,' he said as he left my office. 'She'll enjoy hearing this. Me own a wine bar!'

In early December 1998 I was booked to appear at the Sandon Cabaret Lounge on the outskirts of Liverpool. I was appearing with my then show-business partner Alan Bates, the hypnotist in our show *The Paranormal Experience*. Alan makes the arrangements so I had no idea who ran this club, to me it was just another booking. As I stood backstage doing the sound checks with microphones, I saw a couple coming towards me. I recognised the man but couldn't quite put a name to the face. Then, as he came closer, I saw that it was George Hindley, the plumber, or rather the ex-plumber.

George shook my hand and introduced his wife. 'Do you like my club then, Derek?' he asked.

Only then did I remember the predictions I had made all those years before. 'Great place,' I said, 'but where's the wine bar?'

George was laughing now. 'It's next door, just where you said it would be. This is Standish Street.'

Hearing this made me smile. Then I heard a voice inside my head say, 'Tell him to look out for a new venture in March. It's going to be better than ever.' So I told George exactly that.

The look on his wife's face was a picture. 'Why, fancy that!' she said. 'We're negotiating to buy new premises in the city centre and hope to complete in March.'

Messages in the Spiritualist Churches

We all require a little encouragement from time to time. I know I do. So over the years I have been attending services in the Spiritualist churches around England and Wales to seek guidance and support. The mediums in the Spiritualist churches often give me personal messages concerning things to come.

At the Spiritualist church in Southport in 1988, a medium, Ms Rose, told me she could see a band of stars around my head. 'Hollywood, Derek!' she said. 'You will be in America in years to come.' Of course I found the idea unlikely but I know better than to question what a genuine medium gives me as truth from the spirit world.

In the Spiritualist church in Liverpool later that same year, the medium, Sue Rowlands, told me I was destined to shoot for the stars. Using the same imagery, medium after medium would say to me, 'America, Derek! Go to the USA. You're surrounded by stars.'

In my experience true mediums give only what they receive from the spirit world and I know that spirit guides do not tell lies. They are elevated souls dedicated to helping the human race. As each individual medium has their own guide, it would be extremely unlikely that in the world beyond these guides had put their heads together to play a joke on me. So when I heard all these gifted mediums speaking to me of a future filled with success in Hollywood, of all places, I was thrilled. But when would it all happen? I could hardly wait.

Still wondering about this years later, I recalled I had been on holiday in Spain in 1995 and met a lady there who was a medium. There was a strange synchronicity to our meeting. Gwen and I were staying at a massive hotel and the restaurant must have seated five hundred people. One night we went in and there was no free table. We had to share a table for four with another couple. As soon as I looked at the lady sitting opposite me, I knew she was psychic. She must have seen the same thing I saw, because together we both said, 'You're not, are you?'

The next day this wonderful lady and her husband joined Gwen and me as we walked along the sands. It was then that she gave me a very specific message. There was a man that I had to go and find who would change my life. She said his name was John and he lived in or very close to the Lancashire town of Leyland. She told me I already knew of this man and he would take me to my destination.

As I thought back to her message, the words now returned to me: 'John is linked to America.' I had to find this man. So one night early in 1997 I sat down in my meditation room and asked Sam, my guide, to help me in my search. An image of my friend Alan Bates came into my mind and I knew that he must have the key to this problem.

The next day I contacted Alan and asked him whom he knew called John that had connections to America. Alan suggested the writer John G. Sutton and agreed to introduce me. The rest is, as they say, history.

In my years as a spirit medium, if I have learned one thing it is that when something is meant to happen, it will, but only if we try. The spirit world helps us, but in often very peculiar ways. The one thing we all should remember is that we cannot achieve anything without making a personal effort. Messages of hope from mediums are of use only if we accept and act upon them. Had I not listened to the many mediums who told me about America and then tried to follow it up, things could have been so different. For one thing you would never have been able to read this book – you see, John G. Sutton helped me to write it.

Spirit Rescue

THE HAUNTED RADIO STATION

In the town of Preston, Lancashire, there is a deconsecrated church that is used by one of the county's top radio stations, Red Rose 999MW. This old church, once called St Paul's, is thought by many to be haunted. Staff working there during the hours of darkness have seen mysterious shadows moving and heard footsteps walking across seemingly empty rooms. The late-night talk show host Tony Newman experienced an inexplicable sense that something supernatural was present in and around Studio 2. In May 1998 Mr Newman contacted me and asked if I would be prepared to 'ghostbust' the building. But there was a catch; Tony Newman wanted to broadcast the entire proceedings live on his late-night show.

The early evening of Wednesday 20 May was mild and the roads into Preston relatively quiet. I was feeling calm and quite certain of my ability to deal effectively with any resident spirit I might locate in that old church. My only worry was doing this over the airwaves. In some cases, unwanted spirits can be reluctant to move on. Sometimes this reluctance is expressed through violent disruption, furniture being thrown around, electronic equipment malfunctioning, that kind of thing. If the spook pulled the plug, all the listeners would hear was silence. I had tried explaining this to Tony Newman when he suggested the broadcast, but he wanted to do it.

I parked my car inside the grounds of the former church in what had clearly once been the graveyard. The night shadows were falling fast as I walked to the old stone entrance and rang the bell. There was an atmosphere about the place, it felt strangely still and I could have sworn I saw someone watching me from one of the windows. Thoughts raced through my mind. How many times in the past had young brides crossed this threshold on their way to married life? How many babies had been carried in to be christened? Or the mortal remains of loved ones taken their last journey out into the cold churchyard through this arched door? These stones held memories and they surrounded me now as I stood waiting for someone to let me enter to face whatever it was that waited within.

Inside the reception area Tony Newman had a surprise for me. He had invited one of the country's leading authorities on paranormal affairs, the author and lecturer Joe Cooper. I had read Joe's books on telepathy and many of his regular features in *Psychic News*. Tonight, Tony explained, he was to act as an independent adjudicator. As I shook Joe's hand I admired his tie, dark green with matching soup stains. He told me he was there to observe my work and comment on the proceedings for the listeners. So I not only had a ghost to bust, I was also going to receive a running commentary from Mr Cooper.

The first impressions I received from inside Studio 2 were pleasant enough. Tony opened his show by introducing Joe Cooper and me to the listeners. He explained that he and other staff members at Red Rose Radio had experienced strange phenomena and they thought that the place had a ghost. As he spoke, I knew that Tony Newman was right. My psychic senses picked up a distant whisper from an entity not of this world.

Tony Newman had a roving microphone linked directly to the studio broadcast unit. This meant that we could search anywhere in that old church and still be heard live on air. It was after the midnight news bulletin that we began searching for the ghost of Red Rose Radio. As soon as we left Studio 2 I heard a discarnate voice speak to me. 'Leave me alone,' it said, and at the far end of the central corridor I saw a shadow move.

Joe Cooper was by my side with Tony just behind as we hurried towards the darkness at the end of the hallway. Suddenly I saw what looked like the cowled figure of a monk moving up the old stone staircase at the far end of the former church. 'He's there, Joe!' I shouted and, as quickly as I could, I ran after the phantom.

At the top of the stone steps I stopped and looked across the landing. I could see him now. 'Why are you here?' I asked. 'Who are you?'

The spirit was indistinct in the long shadows cast by the dim lighting, but he was there. I heard him speak to me. 'My name is Jacob Jackson. I lived here.' I could see the face of the ghost now.

Tony Newman was beside me. 'Where is he, where?' He could see nothing in that gloomy corner of what had once been the priest's private room deep inside the church. Joe Cooper was taking copious notes in between staring hard into the shadowy stillness of the night.

'Leave this place and walk into the light!' I told the discarnate entity. At the same time I called upon my spirit guide to come forward and lead this lost soul into the world beyond. I knew that he was trapped here. Sometimes this can happen when a person dies and they feel a close affinity with a certain place. They refuse to leave the area despite being in their spirit body and become a ghost. This particular spirit had obviously been around the old church for many years. Maybe the ghost had been a member of the clergy? Its cloak was tied in the traditional monk's fashion with rope around the waist.

As I watched, a bright light lit up what had once been a beautiful leaded window at the rear of the church. For a brief moment the ghost of the monk stood staring straight into my eyes, then it turned and was enveloped by the brightness. In an instant the spirit of that long-dead monk had moved between this earthly dimension and the next. No more would Red Rose Radio be haunted.

Tony Newman was somewhat bemused by all this as he could see or hear nothing unusual.

Back in the studio we discovered that although neither Joe Cooper nor Tony had heard anything untoward, the listeners had. It seems that as I had spoken to the spirit and watched it passing into the light, a disembodied voice had shouted something indecipherable. That shout had been heard quite clearly on air. Perhaps this was the ghost of Red Rose Radio making its final farewell. For, according to Tony Newman, there have been no further sightings of shifting shadows nor any inexplicable occurrences since that night.

One strange thing did happen following my encounter with the ghost of Jacob Jackson. Tony Newman requested information from any listener who might be able to trace the identity of this spirit being. Subsequently a local journalist called Andrew Atkinson contacted my biographer, John G. Sutton, and sent him a copy of a book he had recently written, *The Mad Monk of Penwortham*. The title refers to a district of Preston only a mile or so from the old church of St Paul's, now home to Red Rose 999MW. According to this book, in the early thirteenth century the local abbot was one Roger Norreis whose debauchery and cruelty to his monks earned him the sobriquet 'the Mad Monk'. Of Jacob Jackson no trace could be found in the book. But who knows, perhaps he was one of the mad abbot's unfortunate monks?

FROM THE DARK SIDE

In every culture of the world many people accept that there are both positive and negative forces. The Chinese tradition refers to the yin and the yang, believing that the universe is constructed of opposing powers that coexist on opposite sides of the cosmic spectrum. In Western society we talk of the good force of God and the evil power of the devil. As a medium I know that there is real truth in the belief that a dark side exists, both here on this material plane and in the world beyond. In 1994 I discovered that sometimes entities from the dark side of the spirit kingdom cross through the veil dividing this life and the next, seeking a host body. When this happens, and they succeed, we have what is commonly referred to as demonic possession. In these instances the spirit requiring to be rescued is that of the human being whose body is being possessed.

It was in the unlikely setting of a middle-class suburb of Liverpool that I encountered one of the most clear-cut cases of possession that I have ever seen. The victim was a 23-year-old woman studying law at John Moore's University. (To protect the identities of the people involved, their names have been changed in this account.) She lived at her parent's home and was, before her problems began, as bright, intelligent and respectable a person as one could wish to meet. Her mother and father were proud of their daughter and everyone said she was destined for great things in the legal profession. Until she became possessed by spirits from the dark side.

It was late one November evening that I received the summons to my encounter with the powers of evil. I was preparing to leave my office in Victoria Street when the phone rang. It had been a busy day and I was tempted to let the answering service pick it up, but something made me lift the handset. The desperation in the caller's voice hit me hard.

'Friends gave us your name and number. You must help us! My daughter, our child, it's not Lynn, she's changed . . .'. For a moment the words were replaced with muffled sobs. 'It's not her, Mr Acorah, it's something else too awful to say. Please come and help us, please!'

The address she gave me was on the other side of the river Mersey, miles away from my home. But I had to go. On the way I called in to ask the vastly experienced medium

Kenneth Swindles if he would accompany me. Ken has helped me greatly in the past and I look to him as a kind of personal mentor. Somehow I just knew I was going to need all the help I could get. Being the gentleman he is, Ken agreed at once. Together we set off in my car to see why a young student had suddenly turned into a creature that defied her own mother's description. What we found on the far side of the Mersey that dark night in November will be with me to my dying day.

Mr and Mrs Taylor lived in a large, late-Victorian detached house on the very best side of town. They were an obviously intelligent couple, he a retired merchant sea captain and she a former schoolteacher. But despite their experience and judgement they were both deathly afraid of the daughter of whom they had once been so proud. We were about to discover why.

She was sitting in the main lounge facing the window at the back of the house. Her long black hair hung down past her slim shoulders and she wore a pale-blue dress. The lights were on, yet, as she turned towards us, it seemed too dark to make out her features.

Ken Swindles was standing at my side as I spoke. 'Tell me, Lynn, what is the matter?' I tried to open the conversation gently. Behind me I heard Mrs Taylor weeping.

'She's not here, so piss off and leave us alone!'

For a moment I was shaken, not by the words but by the tone in which they were spoken. Although she was a young woman, her voice was male. 'My name is Derek Acorah and I'm here to help you,' I said, trying to reassure her. It was the eyes that I noticed most, they were shining green like a cat's caught in a car's headlights. I sensed Ken standing close and thanked God that I had asked him to join me.

Lynn rose and approached us. 'Dance with me, Derek Acorah, let me feel your dick!'

I heard a faint cry and the sound of Mrs Taylor fainting behind me as she hit the floor. Ken Swindles touched my arm. 'Ask who speaks,' he said.

'If you're not Lynn, then who are you?' I asked, dreading the reply.

'Why, don't you know, Derek Acorah? *Ich bin von Deutschland, und mein Freund, ich bin nicht allein.*' Ken understood German and translated this for me as 'I am from Germany, and, my friend, I am not alone.' I knew then we were facing evil. Sexual perversion and obscenity predominate on the dark side.

The room seemed cold and my breath misted as I asked again, 'Who are you and why are you here?' A thin smile parted Lynn's lips and spittle dribbled out from the side of her mouth. Ken Swindles was gripping my arm so tightly it hurt. But answer came there none, just a demonic laugh and a mouthful of vile-smelling slime as the thing that was once Lynn Taylor vomited onto the floor.

My stomach heaved as the horrible stench of that vomit filled the room. Behind me I could hear Mr Taylor trying to comfort his wife. Before me stood the physical body of their daughter, but she was no longer in control of it. Something that had escaped from the pit of darkness had taken possession of her, and yes, I was afraid.

Somehow I found the strength to walk up to Lynn. I had to make contact with her to open the invisible door between this world and the next. I had to order out the evil entity that lurked within her body. Ken Swindles walked by my side; he was seventy years old at the time, but a brave man and determined. Together we reached forward and grasped Lynn's arms. They felt strangely powerful.

'Get off, you bald-headed old bastard! Get your filthy hands off!' Lynn's eyes seemed to flash emerald green as she spoke. I had hold of her arm, then she flexed her muscles and almost threw me to the floor with incredible strength.

Ken and I held her between us and together we called on the evil entity within to leave this innocent girl and return to the dark side from where it had come. I could sense my spirit guide Sam with me. In my mind I heard his comforting voice telling me to continue. Both Ken Swindles and I prayed to

God almighty to save this young woman. Slowly she began to relax and suddenly Lynn was asleep.

Mr Taylor helped us to carry his daughter upstairs to her empty room where she now slept. The windows were shuttered and there was no furniture, not even a bed. 'She smashed everything,' Mr Taylor said. Tears ran down his face as he told us what else his poor stricken daughter had done. 'She eats her own dirt,' he sobbed, unable to control his emotions any longer. 'You will save her, tell me you will?'

Back in the main room of the house Mrs Taylor was recovering. Over a cup of tea she told us about her daughter's terrible plight. She said that it all began as Lynn's studies at the university approached a critical point. She had been spending hours and hours continuously studying in her room. One day when Mrs Taylor looked in, the entire place had been wrecked and Lynn was sitting silently in the corner, completely naked. They had called their doctor, who had prescribed tranquillisers, but Lynn, or rather the thing within her, would not swallow them. She had been gradually worsening ever since. Eventually the doctor had diagnosed schizophrenia. He wanted to have Lynn certified and placed in a secure mental hospital, but her parents were reluctant. Instead, Mr Taylor had called in the local vicar, who also said it was a medical matter. Now they were at their wits' end.

Having seen and heard the entity within Lynn Taylor, I was certain she was possessed. Her only hope of salvation seemed to be spiritual cleansing. That thing within her had to be vanquished. Kenneth Swindles and I promised to return the following evening to repeat out attempts to banish the evil entity occupying her body. What neither of us knew then was that there were more than one of them.

The following day Ken and I arrived early and we were shocked to see the Taylor's house in daylight. The previous evening's darkness had hidden the extent to which Lynn, in her possessed state, had damaged the property. All the downstairs front windows had been smashed and covered

over with boarding. To prevent her escape, the Taylors had
fitted metal bars to the windows. It looked more like a
Victorian jail than a respectable private residence. We
knocked and Mrs Taylor opened the door. She was in a terrible state and clearly hadn't slept. 'There's someone else in
her now,' she said, 'another voice, I heard it this morning.'

Lynn was lying in the far left corner of her room, staring
straight ahead. The stink of human excrement was overpow-
ering, and bits of this were smeared around her mouth.

'*Ich gehe saugen dein Pimmel*, Derek Acorah!' (I'm going to
suck your dick.) Again she spoke in German, this time with a
female voice. Quickly Ken and I walked forward and placed
our hands firmly upon her arms and shoulders. I felt her
shuddering violently and called upon my spirit guide to
come and take this evil entity away from the victim. The
room was freezing cold though outside the weather was quite
mild for late November. Ken was praying out loud and I
tried to follow his words.

Suddenly Lynn relaxed completely. She went totally limp
and slumped down to the floor. For a second I thought she
had fainted. But then she looked up and saw her father in the
doorway. 'What's happening?' she said. 'Who are these
people?'

I almost cried with joy; the young woman was back in
control of her body. She had returned from the abyss, at least
for the moment.

But it took almost two months of repeated visits to rid
Lynn of her demons. During those months we saw many
other evil entities presenting themselves. One by one our
own spirit guides drove them out of that poor lady and back
into the dark regions of the spirit realms from where they
had escaped.

Today Lynn Taylor is fully recovered and has resumed
her legal studies. But it could have been so different had her
parents not sought help outside the sphere of medical care.
As a medium I know that there are powers which may exceed
the current extent of human understanding. Of course no

one should wantonly refuse a competent medical diagnosis, but doctors themselves can only operate within the boundaries of their knowledge. Certainly no physician that I have ever heard of would prescribe any form of spiritual exorcism. Yet doctors may, and often do, prescribe a severely debilitating drug regime, secure mental institutions and even electro-convulsive therapy (ECT). This despite the fact that even they do not know why, in some few cases, it works. Perhaps ECT is part of medical mythology?

The frightening case of Lynn Taylor proved to me that demonic possession is not simply spiritual mythology. At certain times conditions prevail that enable dark forces to join together and become capable of invading a vulnerable human being. On very rare occasions these manifest themselves in a case of possession. However, the powers of darkness cannot overcome the powers of light. For Lynn, the long dark night of suffering has ended. For others the hell goes on.

Messages for the Rich and Famous

During my psychic career I have met many rich and famous people. They are very often interested in my work and it has been my pleasure to offer my services as a spirit medium to them. I am obviously not going to breach any delicate confidences that were passed to me from the spirit world, but here are some examples from the pages of my celebrity autograph book.

In 1990 I was visiting my sister in Michigan, USA, and she invited me to go to a Lionel Ritchie concert with her. I like Lionel's music so of course I said yes. The venue was called The Dome and it was packed with thousands of people. By chance, or fate, our seats were directly behind those of the film star Burt Reynolds.

Lionel Ritchie came on and began his show. He has a wonderful voice and a tremendous stage presence. I was really enjoying myself when I suddenly became aware of a Native American standing just to the right of Burt Reynolds. I knew this was not a physical being, as my sister sitting next to me would have certainly noticed. Then I heard a voice saying to me, 'Tell him he's being offered a big, important film that is going to be at the Oscar ceremonies,' and I could see that this spirit meant Burt Reynolds.

At the interval I tapped Mr Reynolds on the shoulder and told him his spirit guide had a message for him.

He looked at me as though I were a loony. 'Really?' he said and edged towards the aisle.

'The large Red Indian that's been standing here says you have an Oscar-nominated role coming up.'

I have to say this for Burt Reynolds, he never blinked. 'Oh yes?' he said. 'And who are you?' When I told him, he invited me to join his party and tell him more. There was, of course, lots more. Burt was an absolute gentleman and I told him many things about his forthcoming successes. These predictions have subsequently come true. He was nominated for an Oscar for his part in the film *Boogie Nights* in 1998.

Back in the days when I was living in Australia and playing for USC Lion, I was travelling to Sydney from Adelaide. In the first-class section of the plane I found myself seated next to Bette Midler, the singer and actress. Bette was in Australia on tour. As we spoke, I got the impression that she was psychic herself. When I mentioned this, she agreed with me and said that over the years she had had a number of paranormal experiences.

Bette Midler was at the time in a personal relationship with a gentleman that was not right for her. I could see very clearly the man she would eventually marry and he was not around her yet. I also saw that Bette would be the mother of a beautiful baby girl and this child would have her mother's talents. In the later years of her life Bette Midler would give large sums of money to help needy causes in and around the area of her home. When I told her all this, Bette just smiled.

She is now married, with a daughter.

In London for a long weekend break in 1991, Gwen and I were dining at the Inn on the Park in Park Lane. There I met the singer and film actress Cher. As we spoke, over a glass of wine, I saw that this lady was a very sensitive soul. She may appear to be self-confident but I could see that Cher had a tendency to worry far too much. Cher's spirit guides are always close to her and she is, I know, often aware of their presence. They are there to support and help her through the very active and high-profile life she leads. She would have to overcome a great sadness in her life, I could see.

Cher must have been reasonably impressed by what I told her, because she gave me a ring as a thank-you present. Today it is one of my most treasured possessions.

Dionne Warwick, the singer, was performing in Southport, Merseyside. The stage manager at the Southport Theatre is a friend of mine and invited me to meet Dionne, who had been told about my psychic powers. So after the concert, I had the privilege of being introduced to her.

As we sat backstage, I suddenly saw a clear vision of her in Brazil. Dionne was going to move there, I knew that. When I told her what I had seen, she confirmed that she had indeed been thinking of setting up home there and was amazed that I had seen this.

The move away from America was, for Dionne, tinged with a little sadness. She had experienced some rather unpleasant attitudes there and wanted to live in peace. I just knew that Brazil was absolutely the best place for her.

I also gave Dionne a consultation over the phone. As we spoke I could see a vision of her son and realised that to Dionne Warwick this young man meant the world. I sensed also that he had a true and natural talent that would, in years to come, be recognised.

Dionne confirmed all I told her, and yet I knew that there was more for her to do in this life. She herself knows this and in the future will be instrumental in setting up aid facilities for deprived people.

Granada Breeze Satellite Television in England hired me for a series called *Livetime* which is a magazine-style chat and feature show screening in the afternoon across Europe. In

December 1998 it was going out from the London studios of Granada and I was there with the film actor George Hamilton. Before the start of the show, Sam, my spirit guide, said to me, 'Ask him about his good-luck charm. He was given it in America just before he left.'

This elicited a questioning look from George. 'You're right, but how do you know?' he asked, clearly a little suspicious. Then he pulled a small talisman from his trouser pocket and showed it to me. 'A spiritual friend of mine gave me this just before I left America to fly here,' he said.

When we were live on camera, I was invited to tell George Hamilton more. I could see a vision of George with crystals and told him this. Sure enough, he was wearing crystals around his neck. Then I had a vision of his future home, a huge, white-painted house. When I told him this, he laughed, thinking I was talking about the White House. But he is not about to run for president.

It was great fun on that Granada show and I know Mr Hamilton enjoyed it too. Though I suspect he still wonders how I knew about his talisman.

Working for Granada TV I meet lots of famous people. The studios in Quay Street, Manchester, are buzzing with celebrities filming various programmes. One famous lady I had the pleasure of working with was the delightful Julie Goodyear, who was for some twenty-five years a leading member of the cast of the British drama *Coronation Street*. Julie was presenting *Livetime* for a month in January 1999 and she really captured my heart with her kindness. On camera Julie is the ultimate professional and helped me tremendously. But off camera she couldn't wait to hear what I had to tell her.

Backstage Julie Goodyear and I sat together while I tuned in to her vibrations. For Julie I saw many important new TV contracts, brilliant offers, even one from the BBC. I also saw a vision of Julie in my home town of Liverpool being toasted as some kind of community leader.

Seven days later I opened a copy of the *Liverpool Echo* and there, smiling out at me, was a huge picture of Julie Goodyear who had just become an honorary cultural ambassador of the City of Liverpool.

Testing My Psychic Powers at the International Society for Paranormal Research in Hollywood

Meeting the ISPR Team

Throughout my life I have been aware of the psychic powers that I was born with. To me these are a natural part of my everyday existence. Yet many people deny that the psychic gifts I possess actually exist. Almost daily I hear sceptics say such things as 'utter rubbish, he's just a clever con man'. To myself I have nothing to prove. I am secure in the perfect knowledge that what I give from the spirit world is exactly what I receive. I trust my guide Sam completely and he always tells me the truth. But I recognised that for many my word was not proof enough. So to expel all doubts about my veracity I decided to put my personal psychic powers to the test. And in January 1999 my biographer, John G. Sutton and I, with our wives Gwen and Mary, flew out to California.

The parapsychologist Larry Montz PhD is the head of the International Society for Paranormal Research (ISPR), whose headquarters are in Los Angeles. There we were to meet Dr Montz and undertake a series of scientific investigations designed by the ISPR to test my psychic and mediumistic powers. This visit turned out to be an incredible experience that has changed my life forever.

Dr Montz has been investigating the paranormal for over twenty-seven years and he works with a team of scientists and some of America's top psi investigators. They work in the field, not in a laboratory. If Dr Montz, who has a degree in psychology from Trinity College, Cambridge, said I was the real thing, then surely no sensible person could reasonably doubt it. So on 9 January 1999 we set off to find out. I must admit I was just a little nervous. Though I had, as I always have, great faith in my spirit guide Sam. He was with me as I walked the first few steps into America. 'Big things for you now,' he said.

Both Dr Montz and Daena Smoller, the ISPR executive officer, met us at the airport. Dr Montz is big and powerfully built. An air of self-confidence exudes from him. His dark, very American looks are matched by his firm handshake and deep voice. 'Cool,' he said, taking my hand. He told us to call him Dr Larry.

Dr Larry drove us to our hotel in Santa Monica. Our room was number 306, the same number as my office in Liverpool. To me that was a sign that I was on the right track. As I turned to shake Dr Larry's hand and thank him for his kindness, he gripped my arm and looked deep into my eyes. 'We've waited years for you, we knew you were coming,' he said. This was no chance meeting, this was destiny.

There was no time to admire the beach and the palm trees, because Dr Larry had agreed with one of his ISPR team members to begin my testing the next morning. The first test was to assess my clairaudient ability on a nationwide phone-in programme. The distance between me, in my hotel room in Santa Monica, and the callers, selected at random, could be anything up to 4,000 miles. The first test was to commence at 8 a.m. during a fifteen-minute interview with Linda Mackenzie of the ISPR on her show *Creative Health and Spirit*. At 7.55 a.m. John arrived at my door to make sure I was ready to do the broadcast. But when I dialled the number I had been given, a prerecorded voice said, 'The number you have called has been disconnected.'

John had contact numbers for Daena and Dr Larry, but at Daena's house only her answerphone picked up the call. John finally got through to Dr Larry and was provided with a new number from Linda Mackenzie's producer. At approximately 8.25 a.m. I was through to the radio station and broadcasting across the USA and even Canada.

Soon I was linked to callers telephoning the station from all over the USA. One lady who called had been thinking about moving house. I could hear my spirit guide Sam saying, 'Tell her she moves in August.' When I did, the response was an amazed 'How do you know? That's exactly when we planned to move! You are so right!'

Afterwards, I was pretty sure I had passed my first test.

Daena and Dr Larry came to the hotel to pick us up for brunch. I had never heard of brunch but I was certainly hungry. Outside I was introduced to Linda Mackenzie, the radio host from this morning's show, and her business partner Barbara Savin. Linda looked like a blonde film starlet and was driving what to me seemed like a hot-rod sports car. Well, this was Hollywood! Dr Larry explained that at Mel's Diner we would meet his other ISPR team members including one of America's leading psi investigators, Peter James.

As we approached Mel's Diner on Sunset Strip and turned into the car park, I saw a man with long grey hair and a vivid black moustache standing by the entrance. I knew at once that this person had paranormal powers; his aura was extremely bright and seemed to melt into infinity. 'Is that Peter James?' I asked Dr Larry. He smiled and replied, 'You know it is.'

Inside, I sat next to Dr Larry with Peter James on my left. I could feel he was tuning in his psychic senses and trying to assess myself and John G. Sutton. 'Come on then, Peter, tell us what you see?' said John.

Mr James looked ever so slightly taken aback. 'You write books,' he replied, 'very successful best-selling books, and you are walking a pathway to the very top.' That was Peter James's prediction for John. It certainly made him smile.

Over the food and coffee we got to know the ISPR team members. Ron Kilgore, a big, friendly guy, is a radio presenter and ISPR scientific investigator. Dr Larry explained the day's programme. We were going to conduct an investigation into the Comedy Store, a Hollywood club whose owner, Mitzi Shore, had been the driving force behind many top comedians, such as Robin Williams and Richard Pryor. Her club had previously been investigated by the ISPR and they had knowledge of the discarnate entities thought to haunt this old building. My test was to identify them by name and, as the ISPR had previously checked the history, whatever I came up with could be verified against their records.

THE HAUNTED COMEDY STORE

The full ISPR team arrived at the Comedy Store on 8433 Sunset Boulevard around 1 p.m. Dr Larry was carrying a magnetometer to measure any fluctuations in the electro-magnetic energy field, and a 35mm camera. The ISPR scientific investigators were Shawn Roop with a digital camcorder and Ron Kilgore with a highly sensitive audio-cassette recorder. The ISPR psi investigators were Daena Smoller, who also had an electronic temperature gauge, Peter James and Linda Mackenzie. And then there was me, the subject of this test. I was a little nervous, but my guide Sam was with me and he wouldn't let me fail.

As we were preparing to enter the club, Dr Larry sprang a surprise on us. 'We can't go in yet,' he said. 'This ISPR investigation is being filmed for network TV by the E! Entertainment Channel.' As he spoke, a number of cars drew into the car park carrying the crew and their cameras. Soon we were giving interviews about our personal expertise and paranormal powers.

The day was warm and the sun was shining in a clear blue

sky outside the Comedy Store, but as I looked towards the entrance I saw a cold figure. It was the spirit of a former cabaret dancer motioning to me to walk towards her. A chill ran down my spine. Whatever spirits waited within that black-painted building knew we were coming. They were expecting us. I glanced across at Peter James. 'I'm scared of ghosts!' he said to make me laugh. But the spirit of the long-dead girl was still standing in the dark doorway. There was something sinister about her faded smile, and the hairs at the nape of my neck tingled.

As Dr Larry led the ISPR team into the club I felt my spirit guide move closer to my side to protect me. His near-ness made me feel quite safe, even when an unseen hand brushed icy fingers through my hair and a husky voice chuckled in my ear, 'This way, honey.' It was some discar-nate spirit of the night welcoming me as a customer.

We passed through a corridor lined with huge photographs of famous comedians who had featured at the Comedy Store. There were many big names, such as Pauly Shore and Jim Carey. They stared sightless from the walls into the shadows of the club, which had once been known as Ciro's and a Mafia haunt. In another dimension it still was, as we were about to discover.

The dark corridor opened out into the main cabaret lounge, which consisted of a semicircular stage surrounded by round tables with bow-backed chairs. On the black-painted walls were white stylised images of the Marx Brothers. A shiver of nervous excitement rippled through my body as the atmos-phere enveloped me. The entire premises seemed highly charged and I knew that many spirits were present. Then Linda Mackenzie ran forward to the side of the stage. 'Over here!' she called. 'He's on the stage!'

Dr Larry was beside Linda in an instant and soon the full ISPR team were there on the stage, tuning in to the entity she had detected.

'Temperature's fallen five degrees,' Daena Smoller reported.

'Magnetometer active . . . very active!' shouted Dr Larry, who was right in the centre of the cold spot. Instantly the whole club became noticeably cooler. The TV camera team looked slightly shocked as they too became chilled by the unseen presence.

'Smell the smoke here!' called Peter James as he stood beside Daena. 'Cigar smoke, can you smell it?' he said, and I could.

The name Frank sprang into my mind. 'Francis . . . Frank they called me,' I could hear this entity calling to me. 'Why are you here? Why?' I knew then that we were not welcome. Whoever Frank had been, he wasn't used to uninvited guests.

Daena was trembling slightly as the power of this invisible spirit entered her space. She is an incredibly sensitive medium and discarnate entities can sometimes overpower her. I called on my guide Sam to help. He did, reaching out from the spirit world to protect both me and my new friends. 'He's gone, you're safe,' Sam said to me. But the club was still very cold. Out of the corner of my eye I saw a dark shadow edging through a door at the far end of the room.

'I was murdered,' said a distant female voice. 'They killed me, but I'm not dead!'

All the time Dr Larry was watching me very closely. Was I passing this test, I wondered?

Peter James too had sensed the presence of the murder victim. He led the way with Dr Larry close behind, followed by myself, the rest of the ISPR team and a very bemused TV producer with her crew. Slowly we followed the still invisible entity into a dimly lit room behind the stage. Then the pain of that spirit's death hit me deep inside, and for one ghastly moment I was in the 1930s in the body of a dying woman. Agony surged through me; my stomach and all the lower half of my body seemed to burn with the intensity of the injury that the poor lady had suffered. 'They killed my baby too,' said that lonely, long-ago voice. 'We died here in this room.' I nearly screamed in terror as the utter helplessness of this victim of a failed abortion spoke to me from across the decades.

Linda Mackenzie looked around and seemed to see something moving upwards and outwards. As she did so, I felt the spirit lift away from me, and relief flooded through. For a moment tears pricked my eyes as the last remnants of her despair rocked my consciousness. She didn't want to die! She was young, she had her life. These things I knew. Then Dr Larry took my arm, 'Are you OK, Derek?' he asked, and the firmness of his strong but gentle voice comforted me.

Turning, Dr Larry led us back into the main cabaret lounge. We crossed to the far left and gathered together.

'Get off! Don't *do* that! Get *off*!' Linda shouted, straightening her skirt. 'This is a rude spirit!' she said.

I heard a voice in my head; 'Gus,' it said. 'I'm Gus.' I spoke the name out loud.

'Yes, we know that name,' said Dr Larry.

Peter James was almost dancing on the spot. 'He likes Linda, oh yes, he likes her,' Peter said. But Linda said nothing, she just held tight on to her skirt. 'This man worked here, he carried a gun,' Peter said. 'Big man, he was a guard of some kind. But he liked the ladies!'

Linda Mackenzie dodged to the right and glared at Peter. 'You're telling *me*!'

In the far corner of the club I sensed another discarnate spirit. Then it called to me as though to an old friend. 'I was handsome too, you know?' said the ghost of a young man. 'Just like my father.' I repeated what I had heard.

'Ask for a name,' said Dr Larry in a cool and commanding tone, and I was aware that this was part of my examination.

Listening with my mind, I heard the spirit speak again. 'Why, they called me Sean, Sean Flynn. I used to come here, I like it here.' Giving this name and information to Dr Larry, I looked closely into the darkness. There were only shadows and an invisible being.

'Temperature down nearly ten degrees!' said Daena.

For a brief instant I saw this spirit in my mind's eye. He

was indeed very like Errol Flynn, with aquiline features, athletic build, and so proud in the former glory of his long-dead body. 'I was killed, you know, but I still come here. Ha! Ha!' The ghost of Sean Flynn laughed. 'This week my father's name will be news all over the USA,' he said. Then the ghost spoke to me of a tragedy to come: 'Earthquake, it happens in June, thousands killed, devastation.' I repeated what I heard this spirit speak in my mind.

'Not so!' Linda Mackenzie shouted. 'This is not going to happen!'

I was shocked now. The ghost of Sean Flynn had gone. As it turned out, his prediction of earthquake was just a nasty joke he had played on me. No doubt in life Sean had been something of a prankster and his joking had not stopped with his physical death.

Within a room off the central area I saw quite clearly the spirits of two dancing girls in their dark dresses and fishnet stockings. Briefly they high-kicked and spun around as they no doubt had done decades ago. They looked happy and the whole feel of the place changed as they danced before me. Suddenly I wanted to dance too. What an incredible place the Comedy Store is! Especially for someone with developed paranormal powers.

Outside in the California sunshine, Dr Larry called the ISPR team together for a debriefing session. Only Linda and I had never been near the place before and we had no knowledge of the ISPR's previous findings concerning this property. Dr Larry told us that he was quite astounded with the results of this investigation because they matched so closely those from the previous ISPR team. I had correctly given the known names of spirit entities identified by Peter James and other ISPR team members in the past.

My biographer was standing at my side. 'And what do you think of Derek Acorah now, Dr Larry?' he asked.

Dr Larry raised his eyes and said, 'Cool, John.' To my ears that was praise indeed.

THE PINK MANSION

The following day the full ISPR team took me up to Cresthill Road, high in the Hollywood Hills. There we were to conduct an investigation into a pink-painted mansion that had once been the home of Jerry Lewis, the 1950s comedian. In recent years this house had been used by numerous comics while they were booked to perform at the Comedy Store. Many, such as Sam Kinnison and Andrew Dice Clay, had reported seeing ghosts or mysterious moving shadows within this weird Spanish-style mansion. According to Pauly Shore, Mitzi's son, there had been lots of celebrities living there in the past and the place was associated with such names as Dean Martin and Sammy Davis Jr. These powerful personalities were certain to have imprinted their energy on the premises.

As soon as we arrived, radio and TV news crews and reporters surrounded us. The ISPR had really captured the imagination of the US media with this mission. They all wanted to know what we expected to find within the walls of the pink mansion. In a quiet moment I asked my spirit guide Sam that very question. 'Nothing to fear,' he said, 'only old memories.'

Inside the heavy oak and iron door of that mysterious mansion, my first impressions were totally happy ones. I could sense the joy that those long-ago Hollywood stars had felt in this home. Here there had been parties, late nights, loud music and all the excesses that Tinsel Town had to offer. The walls had once been hung with expensive paintings from great artists such as Picasso and van Gogh. In my mind I heard echoes of distant laughter coming down the years. Yet there had been tears too. This was a house with a history and we were going to discover it.

Peter James was the first to speak: 'Samuel or Samuels was here, I hear the name clearly.' We were standing on the stairs when Peter spoke again. 'There is a vortex here,' he said.

'Temperature falling fast,' Dr Larry reported.

Suddenly I saw blood forming before my eyes; it pooled into a dark crimson mass on the stairs leading down into the depths of the pink mansion. 'Shot here!' I shouted, but it was not my voice, it was almost as though I were taken over by some unseen being. My forehead hurt terribly. 'Shot in the head!' I said, and then I saw a vision of the body of the murdered man lying lifeless on the stairs where he had fallen many, many years before.

The camera crews too were experiencing the rapid fall in temperature. Further into the mansion Linda Mackenzie discovered a particularly cold spot. This was just inside what was now the kitchen area. 'Two women died here,' she said.

Peter James was alongside Linda. 'They died in this very room,' he said.

I could sense the sadness of those long-dead women. Daena Smoller could too, she was almost in tears beside me. The high emotion of those final moments had etched itself into the fabric of this old house. Because we were super-sensitive we could detect these hidden vibrations, connected with sudden and violent death.

'This mansion was once owned by the Mafia,' said Dr Larry. 'I believe it was a bordello.' That would help to explain the deaths we had sensed with our paranormal powers. Gangsters' molls were expendable.

The investigation over, Dr Larry conducted his customary debriefing. He stated that the electronic equipment had registered positive proof that there had been a number of spirit entities present during our time within the pink mansion. These were most likely fleetingly attracted by the collective psychic forces generated by the paranormally empowered ISPR team. This often happens around mediums, as those in the spirit world see a chance to communicate. To discarnate entities, a gifted medium shines like a bright light of opportunity. These visiting spirits were not malevolent and the property was not actively haunted by any malign entity. However, as previous occupants had noted, it was visited on infrequent occasions by the ghosts of its past.

Turning to Dr Larry, I asked him outright if he was satisfied with my performance. I just had to know! 'Derek,' he said, in his deep, slow, meaningful voice, 'you're still here, aren't you?'

That night we were on practically every newscast throughout California and networked across many other states of the USA. On CBS TV news they introduced the ISPR team as 'the real *X Files* investigators'. Indeed, we were, though I could hardly believe it myself.

THE VOGUE THEATER

At 6675 Hollywood Boulevard, just down from Mann's Chinese Theater, stands the Vogue. This 1930s venue saw many film premieres in its early days. Now it is the headquarters of ISPR. On the evening of 12 January I was to give a public demonstration of my spirit mediumship there. The dynamic Daena Smoller, executive head of business for the ISPR, had invited many important figures in the world of film and television to watch me undertake this further test of my paranormal powers. I stood outside and looked up at my name displayed in lights: England's DEREK ACORAH it said. My heart picked up a beat as I stood there on the star-spangled pavement. I had never even dared to imagine this magic moment.

Dr Larry took me upstairs to my dressing room, which had been the projection area when the Vogue was a cinema. As I began to prepare myself for the stage, I saw something glittering by the side of my folded jacket. It hadn't been there seconds earlier, when I had placed my stage clothes down, of that I was quite certain. I picked up the object; it was a shimmering American dime. I showed this to Dr Larry and John, who was also with me.

'We find money all the time in this theatre,' Dr Larry said. 'It seems to drop out of thin air.'

'I found one too,' John said, and pulled from his suit

pocket a one-cent coin. 'It's dated 1976, the year my dear daughter Dulcie Jane was born.'

As I walked down the stairs leading to the main auditorium, I felt sure this was going to be a great success. I heard the sound system announcing me – 'Please welcome Derek Acorah!' – and I was on stage.

My first message from the spirit world was to a delightful blonde lady called Donna. She was clearly pregnant and I asked if she would like me to tell her the sex of her child. I heard Sam, my guide, say, 'Tell her it's a beautiful baby boy.' When I gave this information to her, she confirmed that medical tests showed the same. I then heard Sam say, 'Eight pounds ten ounces.' I gave this weight to Donna as a prediction. Then I heard the name Steven and passed this to her.

'You couldn't have given me a name closer to my heart!' she said. 'That's my boyfriend, the father of the baby!'

Both Donna and Steven were producers with the ABC TV network based in Hollywood. I could see only success and happiness for them.

Towards the right centre of the theatre I saw a lady with a really powerful aura. It shone so brightly, that I couldn't help but speak to her. It turned out that she was Marilyn Sinatra, the niece of Frank Sinatra. Perhaps personality-plus runs in families. I told her that her guides in the spirit world had been watching her making major alterations in her Beverly Hills home. 'You've been changing the kitchen completely,' I told her.

'Why, that's absolutely right!' she replied.

Then I spotted Liz, the producer from the E! Entertainment TV channel. Above her head I could see a sparkling diamond ring, and as I looked, I saw a vision of a handsome young man placing this upon her finger. 'You will be engaged to be married within six months,' I told her. 'Then you'll have the most lovely twin children.'

She gasped aloud when I said this. 'There are twins in my family,' she said.

'Well, there will soon be two more,' I told her. Sam was sure.

The wonderful audience at the Vogue Theatre just couldn't have been kinder to me. Afterwards I discovered that I had given messages to many high-powered TV and film executives. As we prepared to leave the Vogue Theater, Dr Larry asked me to speak to a man from Dotted Line Entertainment Inc. There was something about this man that brought the image of a robotlike being from another planet into my mind. How odd! I thought. He looks human enough! But I decided to mention it to him.

'Oh yes!' he said. 'I'm one of the creators and producers of the award-winning children's TV series *Field Trip*, which features two friendly aliens from another dimension.'

So I rather think I passed that test, if indeed it was one. I couldn't be certain where the inscrutable Dr Larry was concerned.

VISITATION AT EDIE'S DINER

Early the next morning I woke and walked out alone onto the beach at Santa Monica. The sea air cleared my mind of the hangover I had from the night before, when John and I had celebrated with a bottle of whisky. The sky was blue, the sea was calm, and looking across the pale sands I could see a film crew setting up for a day's shoot. I knew this was where they filmed *Bay Watch* and wondered if it was for that programme. I felt wonderful.

Edie's Diner stands on the quayside overlooking a harbour bobbing with seagoing boats and motor-powered million-dollar cruisers. From where I was sitting, the boats were only a few feet away. The scent of the sea drifted over me, and high in the sky a gull floated, supported by the rising thermals. We had gathered for a last meal with our new friends Daena and Dr Larry. In the short time that we had known each other, a bond had formed between us. I felt I could trust

these people absolutely and it had been such good fun that I
didn't want it to end.

Suddenly I became extremely cold and aware that a presence was with me. A sense of absolute joy flooded through
me. I could have shouted in divine delight as a feeling of pure
love spread over me. Great tears ran down my face. I was at
one with a force so utterly compassionate and beautiful, a
spirit entity so evolved, that to be there with it was too much
for me. I was trembling now, shaking and crying and
weeping aloud. I could see Dr Larry and John before me but
their faces were obscured by bright shimmering arrows of
pure white light.

'Michael is here,' I heard myself say. 'You two, you are
surrounded by light. Spirit arrows about you, pointing at
you. You must bring truth and light to the world. Michael is
here. He loves you.' Then I took Dr Larry in my arms and
cried like a child with ecstatic joy.

When I looked again, I saw that Dr Larry was wiping away
tears from his own eyes. I felt elated, I had been visited by
the most highly evolved being I had ever encountered. Daena
Smoller was crying now. She seemed in shock. John was
silently staring at Dr Larry and I could see he too was deeply
moved. Our wives Mary and Gwen were looking at each
other as though they didn't know what to say.

'I believe that my spirit guide is called Michael,' Dr Larry
said. 'Sometimes I too feel him beside me as you have just
done. I think that today we have been visited by this spirit
for a specific reason, to tell us we are walking on our predes-
tined pathway.'

And I knew that this was so. Michael had come to me with
that simple message for Dr Larry and also for John to tell
them that they were to be instrumental in bringing the infinite truth of eternal life and love to the people of the world.

'Well, I've never seen Derek do that before!' Gwen said to
Mary.

We all knew that there at Edie's Diner on the quayside at
Marina del Rey we had witnessed something that very few

people in this world ever experience. I was still overcome by the love of that visiting spirit whose name was Michael. I knew then that Dr Larry was a very special person. He had been chosen to undertake a mission to tell the world the truth of life eternal. I also knew that we were meant to be together on this mission. Somewhere in the spirit world, forces beyond our understanding had brought us together. This was only the beginning.

Before we left Edie's Diner, John turned to Dr Larry and asked him outright if he and the rest of the ISPR team had reached a conclusion concerning the veracity of my psychic powers. Dr Larry looked John straight in the eyes and said, 'Derek's clairvoyant ability has stunned me.' And in a way it had stunned me too; I had been changed and enlightened. Now I could see the truth more clearly than ever before in my life.

THE SPIRIT AT THE AIRPORT LOUNGE

We were sitting in the coffee shop, outside the boarding gate when John began to shake. I could see him trembling and immediately sensed that a discarnate entity had entered our space. 'My back, Derek. It's all over my back, freezing cold!' John stood up and I could see a shining around him. 'Now moving over me, Derek, DEREK!'

Mary moved closer to him. 'He's surrounded by coldness,' she said. Gwen stepped forward and I saw she too was registering the dramatic drop in temperature. I could feel it edging out from around John, who was keeping remarkably calm.

Everyone in the coffee shop was staring at us. An old couple some few tables away jumped up and almost ran out of the place.

'Derek, what is this? What's happening to me?' I could see that John was totally enveloped in the spirit's force field, it had engulfed him. I stepped into the shimmering aura around John and shared the experience. It was an entity as powerful and evolved as the spirit of Michael that I had encountered at Edie's Diner earlier. In fact I felt it could be Michael, but this time the visitation was for John.

John's eyes seemed to be focused elsewhere and I knew he was seeing something that did not exist in this material dimension. 'It's OK, Derek,' he said at last. 'I know now, I'm fine.' Then he sat down slowly, trembled and reached out for my hand. 'You know too, don't you?' he said. And of course I did.

The spirit had now moved on. And as though it had never been, the coffee shop returned to its usual temperature, all was as before. But for John and me it wasn't, nor can it be ever again. For we have both encountered at first hand the infinite power of love. From high in the distant realms above, evolved spirits reached down and touched us and from that day on we are both changed forever.

'Nothing can stop us now, Derek,' John said. And I knew that he was right. Nothing was going to prevent us from telling the world the glorious truth that we had both now seen.

PART 2

THE ESSENTIAL GUIDE TO DEVELOPING YOUR HIDDEN POWERS

Your Psychic Potential

INTRODUCTION

Welcome to the section of this book that could change your life. We all have some psychic ability, as you are about to discover, and it is perfectly natural. Some are more gifted than others. To begin with I have devised a simple yes/no test to help you assess your personal potential.

One thing you should always remember is to be totally honest with yourself and all those you are connected with while you test and develop your psychic gifts. They will get better the more you practise, but if you start cheating, the only person you are really defrauding is yourself. I know that you may be tempted to exaggerate or guess when giving information you receive through your psychic powers, but don't do it. Attempts to persuade others that you are tuned in to the world beyond, when you know you are not, can only backfire. So unless you enjoy playing the fool, don't become one by default. It is so easy to do too. Listening in to other people's conversations, picking up on bits of information, then pretending you got this through psychic means – great fun? Oh no, it isn't! It's an insult to your personal integrity.

The key to your psychic development is Truth with a big capital 'T'. Stick to telling that and you won't go far wrong. Be brave enough to admit it if you discover you cannot do something within this development programme. But don't give up too easily. Keep on trying and remember that only by meditation can you achieve the alpha state of consciousness that you must attain to link to your higher self where all knowledge becomes open to you.

These programmes are designed for you and your friends to enjoy. They are not intended to turn you into a psychic super-star. They are simply meant as a gentle introduction to the natural psychic gifts that you were born with but, until now, perhaps never used. Be at peace with yourself as you progress through this easy-to-understand programme. And don't get carried away thinking you are extra special. Just be glad that God gave you these gifts, because He most certainly did.

Test Your Own Psychic Potential

Answer each of the following questions either YES or NO. For each YES answer, score 1; for each NO answer, score 0. Then total your points and refer to the Psychic Potential Assessment below.

	YES	NO
1. Have you ever seen what you believed to be a spirit or a ghost?	☐	☐
2. Have you ever sensed the presence of an unseen person or entity?	☐	☐
3. Have you ever had a vivid dream that eventually came true?	☐	☐
4. Have you ever entered a strange place and imagined you had been there before?	☐	☐

YES   NO

5. From a seemingly empty room, have you ever heard a voice calling your name?

☐   ☐

6. With a close family member or friend, do you ever have telepathic flashes?

☐   ☐

7. Have you ever 'known' something was about to happen, then it did?

☐   ☐

8. When something gets lost in the house, do you find it by intuition?

☐   ☐

9. As a child, did you have an 'invisible' friend that only you could see?

☐   ☐

10. While asleep, do you ever dream you are floating above your bed?

☐   ☐

11. Have you ever had an out-of-body experience?

☐   ☐

12. If you have a pet, do you think it can read your mind?

☐   ☐

13. Do you instinctively know when someone or some place is evil?

☐   ☐

14. In your home, do electrical goods often malfunction when you are close?

☐   ☐

15. Have you ever noticed inexplicable scratch marks on your body?

☐   ☐

YES   NO

16. In your home, have you ever seen
floating globes of misty white light?   ☐   ☐

17. Have you ever had a premonition that
someone is ill or about to die?   ☐   ☐

18. Do you recall your dreams clearly and
in detail?   ☐   ☐

19. Has your home ever filled with a
scent or smell without discernible
trace?   ☐   ☐

20. Have you ever suddenly thought of a
long-lost friend, then they called?   ☐   ☐

Your Psychic Potential Score

15–20   Your psychic potential is very high indeed and it
is highly likely that you could develop your gift to an
advanced level. With this degree of potential you could
progress rapidly, but only if you really want to. Be aware
that psychic powers require great discipline.

9–14   You have above average psychic potential and
could develop your gifts with practice and discipline.
Always remember that only you can open the door, if you
want to.

4–8   Having had some psychic experiences, you may
wish to attempt to develop your hidden abilities further.
Meditation is the key. You must learn to relax into the
alpha state.

0–3   Perhaps you are being too self-critical. However, we
are all psychic so tune in.

A Simple Guide to Meditation and the Alpha State

What is Meditation?

Meditation is state of mind that is relaxed but also alert. During meditation you should aim to be fully aware, yet perfectly calm. It differs from ordinary relaxation in that the consciousness is controlled and not allowed to wander. To achieve this control you must focus the mind in a state of contemplative meditation, also known as the alpha state. This chapter introduces you to the practice of meditation.

Aids to Meditation

From the following list, select an activity to prepare you for meditation.

- Take a warm bath.
- Listen to melodic music.
- Watch the trees and leaves blowing in the breeze.
- Listen to the birds singing in your garden.

- Take a flower and consider the intricate beauty of its petals.
- Gently stroke a pet dog or cat.

If you are now in a mood to meditate, then set aside fifteen minutes to undertake this exercise. Read these instructions through carefully. You will soon learn the sequence as a routine.

HOW TO MEDITATE

This is a simple step-by-step guide to beginning meditation. It is by no means an exhaustive tutorial covering everything, but rather a basic first tutor. If you have never tried meditation, then these exercises are for you.

Controlled Breathing

1. Loosen any tight clothing, necktie etc.
2. Sit with your back well into your favourite chair or lie on a bed.
3. Let your arms rest supported.
4. You must be at ease but not slouched or slumped forward.
5. Listen to your breathing and count the number of breaths you take in approximately one minute.
6. Be aware of your body taking in and expelling air.
7. Breathe out and in slowly and deliberately.
8. Try to slow your breathing rate by breathing more deeply.
9. Continue to control your breathing for approximately five minutes.

Relaxation

You should now be resting, taking deep, regular breaths.

This next exercise should take you approximately five minutes.

10. Imagine your feet are very heavy, they weigh a hundred pounds each.
11. Let the weight fade from you feet. Concentrate your mind on your feet and feel how light and relaxed they become.
12. Now be aware of your legs. They are tense, relax them. Gradually remove that tension from your legs. Be aware of how relaxed they become.
13. Now move your conscious thought to your waist and think yourself up towards your shoulders, easing all the tension out as you do so.
14. Now relax your arms and shoulders. Be aware in your mind of their weight. Ease this away and gently, very gently edge that weight into the atmosphere.
15. Your neck and head now feel so heavy. Just move the weight away, in your mind see it shift into space. You are relaxed.
16. There are now no aches and pains. You have moved them into another dimension. You are now at peace, truly relaxed.

Focusing Your Mind

You should now be relaxed and yet fully aware of your surroundings and of your body.

17. Close your eyes now and count each breath as you take it. Carefully count one to ten breaths, easy, deep and slow.
18. Now, in your mind's eye, imagine a bridge over a river. See that river flowing but look at the bridge. Be aware of the feel, the smell and the sense of this experience.

19. Picture yourself moving towards the bridge. What can you see? Look closely at the water; see the ripples, the trees overhanging the banks of the river. But remember, the bridge is your point of focus.
20. Ignore the sounds of everyday life around you. You are moving ever so gently towards the bridge. Be aware of what you see and look over the bridge to the other side of the river. But do not cross, you are there only to observe.
21. Abandon your thoughts now and sense the other side of the bridge. What can you feel? What can you see? Look and be aware. You are awake and all your senses are alert though you are completely relaxed. You should now be in the alpha state.

Coming out of Meditation

22. Slowly increase your rate of breathing and open your eyes. At this point do not move from your relaxed position.
23. Gently open and close your hands and slowly move your legs.
24. As you become fully awake and leave the state of meditation, be aware of how you feel physically. You may feel slightly elated or tingling as though you have been in a warm shower.
25. Finally stand up, but not too quickly. You have now left the state of meditation.

THE ALPHA STATE

My work as a psychic medium is generally done in the alpha state. By constant and regular practice one can easily achieve this altered level of consciousness, which I believe is the basic essential element of successful mediumship.

In our everyday waking lives our brains have to process

vast amounts of information from countless sources, such as the sound of the radio or TV playing as we try to listen to someone talking to us while the telephone rings and the dog barks. The electrical activity of the brain in such circumstances is between 13 and 30 cycles per second. This is called the beta rhythm. When we relax, sleep lightly or meditate, the rate of our brain frequency reduces to between 7 and 13 cycles per second, and this is the alpha state.

Psychics believe that in the alpha state we feel and sense things that are overwhelmed when we operate in the beta state. The messages are always there but because we are busy in the beta state, we cannot perceive them. To enter the alpha state, we must alter our level of consciousness, for example by meditation.

Experienced psychics can switch quickly from the beta to the alpha state. I can move my consciousness almost at will, but it has taken me years to reach this level of ability. And there are times when even I find it difficult, such as during a period of personal stress. Here are some tips to enable you to begin reaching your own alpha state.

1. First master the art of meditation to recognise the sense of being in the alpha state.
2. Discover what works for you. Some people reach the alpha state by looking at a specific object or listening to a certain piece of music; you must find your own key. Overleaf I have suggested some possible keys.
3. Having found your key to the alpha state, you must learn how to use it to open the door to this altered level of consciousness.
4. Practise looking at your key object or listening to your music in a certain way. Learn to relax and become receptive each time you use your key.
5. Use your alpha state key in conjunction with your daily meditation.

SUGGESTED KEYS AND HOW TO USE THEM

- A small crystal
- A polished stone
- A ring
- The palm of your hand
- Your wristwatch
- A silver coin

Whatever seems right and works for you is fine. Having selected your personal alpha state key, practise the first stages of the meditation process outlined above while looking continuously at your selected object. Try not to blink during this process but don't stare hard, try to gaze gently at your key object. Slow down your rate of breathing, relax and count your breaths as you inhale.

You should feel your level of awareness shifting. Your senses will be more alert and you'll notice that colours seem brighter. Time seems to be moving slowly. Your emotions are stronger, you feel deeply the love you hold for your family. You are now awake in the alpha state.

Once you are able to achieve the alpha state awareness while fully awake, you are ready to proceed to develop your psychic powers.

Opening Your Third Eye

THE PSYCHIC CHANNEL

There is a great deal of utter nonsense talked about opening one's third eye. Some psychic teachers advise students to let their minds become blank. To me, the very idea of a blank mind seems to be a contradiction in terms. Our mind is the very essence of our physical being and controls everything we do, both consciously and subconsciously. Were the mind really to go blank, we would expire. So my first advice to you is to remain alert.

In the previous chapter we looked at a simple method of commencing meditation. In this chapter we'll go on to the next stage: preparing to receive information using our hidden powers. When people talk about being clairvoyant, they are referring to visual information or knowledge received through their third eye. This third eye is identified with the pineal gland. It is dark grey in colour, conical in shape and located behind the third ventricle of the human brain. The French philosopher Descartes thought that the pineal gland was the seat of the soul.

My belief is that the third eye is a very important part of our psychic channel. Through the third eye we may see visions of the past and of the future. It is the pathway to a paradise that lies beyond this physical realm. We should therefore treat it, and all the information and knowledge gathered through it, with great respect.

Note

When beginning this stage of your psychic development, you should not be alone. It is very important that you have others with you for you don't know what you may experience.

The best way to proceed, if you're not a member of a development circle, is to ask your partner or a very close friend to sit beside you. They should not take part in this exercise but be present to support you if so required. They could bring you a cup of tea or coffee, that kind of thing.

This warning is not intended to frighten you, but in any encounter with the unknown, a friend by your side is always going to be reassuring.

STEP BY STEP TO OPEN YOUR THIRD EYE

Before you begin this exercise you should dedicate the experience to your God.

I always say a very simple prayer asking that what I receive be only from the higher levels of the spirit world. Here is a simple prayer of dedication that I recommend to you.

Your Prayer

Dear God, I seek understanding, truth and knowledge only in the divine light of your eternal love.

My Prayer for You

The truth is your divine right. Now prepare yourself to walk forward into the light of understanding. My prayers and my thoughts are with all of you who seek to be enlightened. May your God, our God, the eternal and only God be with you in your quest for now and forevermore.

1. Select a comfortable chair and seat yourself in this. Be relaxed but not slumped forward. Your arms should be supported.
2. Undertake the breathing exercises as outlined in the chapter on meditation. Breathe in slowly and count. Breathe out slowly and count. This will soon become as second nature to you.
3. You should begin to enter the alpha state. If you require an object to concentrate upon, such as a crystal, place this before you now.
4. Once you feel that you have moved to a higher consciousness, relax into the alpha state.
5. Take the forefinger of your right hand (or left if you are left-handed) and place it in the centre of your forehead between your eyes. Now close your eyes.
6. Slowly rotate your forefinger on your forehead in a clockwise direction. You are massaging the pathway to open your third eye.
7. As you gently massage your forehead, imagine you are lifting back a deep purple velvet curtain within your mind. See this curtain, look at the richness of the material and how it shines.
8. Slowly the curtain parts and you see your third eye. It opens ever so gently and it is the most beautiful eye you have ever seen. Look how it sparkles with life and love! This eye is your eye. It sees for you visions you had never before thought possible.
9. Your third eye is now open. Look now with your third eye. You can see. Look at the colours, the

shapes before you. Remember these, be consciously aware of them. You may see visions of faraway places projected as if onto a mirror that may appear to be slightly before your forehead. You are now accessing your psychic channel.

10. Continue to look at the amazing visions you are seeing but do not allow yourself to become locked into this previously unseen world. You are an observer. Simply watch and remember. After no more than ten minutes you must cease this activity.

11. Open both your physical eyes and come slowly out of the alpha state. Remember to undertake your breathing exercises. Breathe in and count, breathe out and count. Gradually you are returning to your normal waking state.

12. Now fully awake, you must close your third eye. This is for your personal protection. You must close your psychic channel. The next chapter describes how to do this safely.

Self-Protection

CLOSING DOWN YOUR PSYCHIC CHANNEL

At least as important as being able to access your psychic channel is the ability to close it down. When I was a young boy of no more than nine, my granny in Bootle, who had been a spirit medium all her adult life, taught me her method. It amounts to protecting oneself. Being fully open psychically and off guard can be quite dangerous. We would not consider leaving the front door of our home swinging wide while we went to bed, would we? But many people developing their psychic powers fail to close them down when they are not being actively used. This can result in unwanted input from discarnate entities just looking for an opportunity to enter your space. Awake and aware you are in control. But should you fail to close your psychic channel down at the end of a period of use, then you really are being very foolhardy.

Consider your psychic ability as one might a radio. To hear anything sensible from the radio, you tune it in to a specific station. If you were to just switch it on, twiddle with the tuner a bit, then walk away and leave it, any station might broadcast. So it is with your powers of perception. You certainly can't watch ten TV stations at once, not properly, so you select one on your television set and watch that. You can't listen to twenty conversations at once during a party, so you concentrate on the person talking to you and listen to them. It is exactly the same with your psychic channel. You tune it in through psychic development, pay attention and it gradually begins to make sense. However, if you do not switch this psychic channel off, it may just be open enough to permit something not wanted through.

By unwanted entities I mean spirits that are seeking to interact with living human beings. Most are harmless and will do nothing worse than whisper silly rubbish. This sort of entity functions on the lowest level, rather like that associated with home-made Ouija boards. They can frighten the unsuspecting by telling them lies that sound like the truth. For example, imagine you heard a discarnate voice say, 'Your mother will die next week.' You might take this seriously. False predictions all come from such entities.

Your spirit guide, on the other hand, will not permit lies to be told to you. However, it is up to you to make certain that you know the difference between your guide and some low-grade entity out to put the spooks up you. There is only one way to do this; be in control and always close down your psychic channels when you don't want them open.

A STEP-BY-STEP GUIDE TO CLOSING YOUR PSYCHIC CHANNEL

1. At the end of each period in which you have opened up your psychic channel, sit for a brief moment and address your higher consciousness.
2. For a second or so, close your eyes and see within your mind your third eye of extended consciousness. It is situated in the centre of your head between your physical eyes and behind the centre of your forehead.

3. You can see your third eye. Now close it and imagine it covered in the most beautiful shimmering purple light.

4. Now, with your physical eyes and your third eye closed, imagine your body being wrapped in a glowing white light. This light will protect you. Nothing can penetrate this immaculate shield of power.

5. You may now open your physical eyes in the firm knowledge that you are completely protected from any unwanted psychic attention.

6. Before you go to sleep at night, repeat this practice, only this time wrap the white light of protection around your home. See your house covered in the glowing white light and sleep at peace in the knowledge that you and all who dwell within are safe.

You must repeat the above exercises each time you finish a period of psychic-level engagement. Do this each time and soon it will become as second nature to you. You may then switch your newly discovered psychic powers on and off at will. Which is exactly as it should be.

Always remember that you are a spirit being incarnate in a physical body and it is your duty to protect that body. So close up your psychic door with the white light of protection and you will be safe. That is what my granny told me almost forty years ago and I have never forgotten. If that is the only lesson you take from this book, then your time has not been wasted. My thoughts and prayers are with you.

PROTECTION AGAINST PSYCHIC ATTACK

It may seem a very fanciful notion but there are people, seemingly ordinary people, who can influence your daily life by attacking you with their psychic powers. Such people are walking in the darkness of this material world and are using their God-given gifts for their own personal gain and self-glorification or gratification. I know personally of self-styled psychic mediums who employ their esoteric knowledge and powers to further their own ends. Some may tell their victims that they are going to enter their minds or visit them in their sleep state. Others conduct dark rites of invocation, calling upon entities resident in the twilight regions between this world and the next to do their evil bidding. This is a frightful misuse of any person's developed psychic powers and eventually it will rebound.

Let me give you an example of a simple, psychic attack. This happens often in everyday life and involves the discharge of negative energy, in the form of thoughts, aimed at you, your family and/or your home. For instance, you have a serious disagreement with a work colleague and they issue insults and maybe even threats against you. These negative thoughts exist in the etheric plane and form themselves into a kind of invisible dagger that, given the opportunity, will tear into the very fabric of your life.

William Shakespeare, the great British poet and dramatist, wrote of such invisible negative forces in lines like 'Is this a dagger which I see before me?' and 'There's daggers in men's smiles'. I think Shakespeare was recognising the fact that thoughts have substance and can kill or injure. If you wish evil on another person and give expression to your thoughts of wickedness, you are creating a negative energy force that has a strange power that is beyond the reasoning of mankind. That such a power exists is attested in mythology and legend dating back to time immemorial. It is from such expressions of negative thoughts that curses come. Serious psychic attacks are a form of curse issued against a person or persons by an individual with enhanced psychical powers and esoteric knowledge.

It is often said that if you do not believe in the mumbo-jumbo of curses and such notions, then they cannot in any way harm you. This is rather like saying that if you do not believe in rain you will therefore not get wet. Being the subject of a psychic attack can result in serious consequences. These could be quite distressing, perhaps even dangerous, if you are unaware that you, or your home and family, are under such an attack.

Here is a list of occurrences that will noticeably increase during a period in which you or a resident family member are under psychic attack.

- Accidents, falls, things being dropped, fires, etc.
- Sleeplessness; waking to strange noises in the night.
- Loss of appetite.
- Feeling of sickness.
- Inability to concentrate.
- Unnatural sexual urges.
- Change of personality.
- Angry outbursts.
- Depression and feeling of worthlessness.
- Feeling of constant unease.

You may, of course, experience any or even all of the above without being the subject of psychic attack. But if you have noticed a serious increase in such unpleasant occurrences, then you might consider conducting a ritual of self-protection that I term a 'candle rite'.

CONDUCTING A CANDLE RITE

Simply follow this step-by-step guide to conducting a candle rite and you will protect yourself and others from any psychic attack.

Equipment

- Four white candles
- Three green candles
- A white sheet

- A bowl of water
- A bowl of salt

1. Place the white sheet on a table or other flat surface.
2. Sprinkle a little water over this sheet.
3. Sprinkle a little salt over this sheet.
4. Place the four white candles in a straight line approximately 12 inches apart.
5. Place the three green candles in a straight line slightly in front of the white ones; they should be approximately six inches apart.
6. Sit in a high-backed chair facing the candles and light them.
7. You should be no more than 24 inches from the row of green candles, seated in an upright position facing them.
8. Now repeat aloud the following prayer of invocation:

Dear God, I pray that you will protect me from harm, from evil and from all thoughts of wickedness that may be directed against myself or those that I love.

Dear God, I pray that you will wrap my body and the bodies of my family and all who live in this house in the protective cloak of your eternal love.

Dear God, please disperse the evil energy and thoughts that may have been directed against all those living within this house.

9. Repeat the above seven times, each time looking closely into the flames of the candles.
10. Having completed this ritual, close with a prayer of your own choice. Or you may use the following:

Dear God, thank you for hearing my prayers. Please forgive those that would trespass against members of my family and myself. Please bring peace and understanding to those who would spitefully use me. And allow me to live in the protection and love of your eternal light now and forevermore.

You have now completed the ritual cleansing of your home and any negative energy that was present will be dispersed.

As you extinguish the candles and return all the equipment to a place of safe-keeping, be aware that this too is a part of the ritual, the final part. Keep your candles and your cloth in a special place ready in case you should require their use again.

The above candle rite works because you are a child of God and are calling upon the hidden powers within and without your physical body to protect you. From the world beyond and also from the world within, you are now protected.

You may use the candle rite to send out love and protection to distant members of your family or friends. Such selfless acts of compassion are especially empowered in the world beyond and the recipients of your kind and positive thoughts will indeed be blessed.

Remember

Hold love and forgiveness in your heart for those who hate and despise you. Do that and you will walk forever in the true light and eternal love of God. My thoughts are with you.

Tuning Your Psychic Powers in to Other People

You will now have developed the ability to enter the alpha state of consciousness and be calm, relaxed and yet aware. This is the essential foundation upon which you will develop your psychic powers. This is not an easy thing that you seek to undertake. Be well aware of that before you start. My thoughts and prayers are with you as you prepare to undertake this onerous task.

Now you are ready to start tuning yourself in to your own psychic powers. If you follow these tutorials and practise them, I can promise you that you will progress towards your full psychic potential. How quickly you progress is entirely with you. There are no short cuts, other than by direct and possibly divine intervention. At the end of each tutorial is a simple test to enable you to assess your progress.

Proceed with hope and love in your heart and you will achieve all you desire. But be aware that if you are simply seeking self-glorification you will ultimately fail. Be honest and truthful with everyone you engage with in your quest to develop your hidden powers and you will succeed.

Dos and Don'ts

- DO NOT give hurtful information to another person, no matter how strongly you feel it to be correct.
  Let me give you an example of information you should NOT give. You are sitting with a subject and sense that their favourite pet is going to die. DO NOT say this to them. It will distress them and they can do nothing to prevent it. Instead say something like 'Your pet loves you a lot and I see it around you.' That's enough.
- DO use your common sense when sitting with any subject. Treat them with respect and always remember that they trust you. This is a very serious matter and you owe them an absolute duty not to betray their trust.
- DO NOT adopt an air of self-importance when speaking to your subject. You are not there to preen yourself and pretend to be clever. Your duty is to tell your subject the truth as you perceive it in a respectful and benign manner.
- DO be positive and caring in your approach to your subject. Anyone who comes to you is seeking good news, not bad news. If you can't give hope, then give all the goodness that is within your heart. Speak the truth gently and temper it with love and understanding. This is a hard world and your duty is to ease the burden of those who may seek your help and guidance.
- DO imagine yourself in the place of your subject. Empathise with them and consider their inner feelings. Be sensitive not only to their hidden information but also to their feelings. Don't spontaneously pass on anything that you receive, or you can utter dreadful messages that hurt.

CLAIRSENTIENCE

This is the psychic ability to sense clearly something about an individual that is not available to you through your accepted five senses. There will be times when this has happened to you spontaneously. If you think carefully about it, you may recall some occasions when this has happened.

Examples of Spontaneous Clairsentience

1. You experienced an instant dislike for an individual, which later proves to have been well founded.
2. You experienced a sense of unease when entering a strange house which later features, or has already featured, in some unsettling occurrence.
3. You see a stranger and immediately feel that they are your kind of person. This eventually turns out to be true and you become good friends.
4. You hear a voice across a noisy, crowded room and search out a friend you have not seen for years.
5. A friend visits and you know at once that they are ill. This proves to be the case though nothing had previously been mentioned.
6. You see a female friend or relation who is pregnant and somehow you know the sex of the child they are carrying.
7. Someone tells you of a new business venture they are entering into and you know that this will be a failure or a success. You are subsequently proved right.
8. A friend telephones you to agree a time to meet and you know that they will not be there. You are subsequently proved to be right.
9. Someone you have trusted for many years tells you a lie and you just know it isn't the truth. You are subsequently proved to be right.
10. A close neighbour tells you they are buying a new

car and you know the colour they have chosen
before they tell you.

If you have experienced any of the above examples, you are
clearly clairsentient. Your ability to sense from others things
that they may not even know themselves is a psychic power
that will serve you well.

HOW TO DEVELOP THE PSYCHIC POWER OF CLAIRSENTIENCE

Clairsentience is one step beyond the instinctive knowledge we
call intuition. Developing this power is rather like learning
to ride a bicycle; we must first trust ourselves. If you recognised a number of the above examples as having happened to
you, then you are well on your way to trusting your own
clairsentient ability. Here is an easy step-by-step tutorial to
enable you to develop your psychic power of clairsentience.

Entering Another Person's Vibrations

Everything in the universe is vibrating. Each single thing, be
it animate or inanimate, has its own level of vibration. This
vibration field is absolutely unique to each individual and no
two people have exactly the same level of vibrations.

You know the sensation of being attracted to someone you
have never met before. As you come close to them you feel an
empathy, a kind of gentle, friendly feeling – good vibrations.
You know also the sense of being repelled by another as their
vibrations clash with yours. Something about this person
puts your guard up at once. You do not feel at ease with
them, bad vibrations in this case.

With clairsentience you are reading from the energy field
of vibrations that surrounds the individual before you. By
using your psychic mind, or higher consciousness, you are
going to access information from their energy field.

There are obvious signs given off by people through their body language. You can note them, but be aware that you are not analysing these as a psychologist would. You are tuning in to the vibration field and seeking knowledge through this. Do not permit yourself to be misled by a person's appearance, either. Some of the most successful people I have met have looked and dressed almost like tramps. To be a true clairsentient channel you must ignore physical appearances and look with your third eye at the 'real' person. It is the truth you are seeking and that cannot be found by allowing your conscious mind to concentrate on outward appearances.

Beginning to Interpret Clairsentiently

To tune in to another person's field of vibrations you must first switch into the alpha state. This is important because it is only through your higher consciousness that you receive clairsentient information. And before you undertake any form of psychic reading for anyone you should always offer a prayer to your God to give you only the truth from the realms of light. Here is a step-by-step guide to beginning to 'read' from another person's energy field of vibrations.

1. Your prayer: Dear God, I seek understanding, truth and knowledge in the divine light of your eternal love.
2. Sit the individual you are reading for down in a comfortable chair opposite your own. The distance between you should be two or three feet.
3. You should be relaxed but not slumped forward and your arms should be supported.
4. Take a series of deep breaths. Inhale and exhale slowly. This will reinforce your alpha state level of consciousness and also fill you with the other person's energy.
5. Open your third eye by stroking the centre of your

forehead in a clockwise direction. Now look immediately above the subject's head and focus your
physical vision in the air around this point.

6. Say out loud all that you see and feel. Do not
consciously weigh the statements you make unless
you feel they are wrong.

7. You will begin to sense certain things about the
subject and you must speak these aloud. For
example, you may get the sensation of being in a
school. Say so – this person may be a schoolteacher.
Be confident in your approach.

8. Let the thoughts flow as they enter your mind and
speak them. If you see or sense a dog or cat, or a car,
say so. You are tuning in to the energy field of this
subject and they will have many influences around
them within that field.

9. Be sensitive to the feelings you receive from the
subject. Talk about these and be as specific as you
can.

10. Express all your thoughts about the subject aloud.
But remember that you are dealing with a sensitive
human being and you must not say anything to
cause them needless distress.

ENTERING ON A VOICE VIBRATION

You may have heard psychics and mediums giving demon-
strations of their paranormal powers on the radio. Listeners
telephone the radio station and are connected to the medium
or psychic who then proceeds to give them a reading. They
do this by linking in to the caller's voice vibrations.

You will quickly recognise how to tune in if you think
about the way a voice fluctuates in tone. For example,
someone who is very angry has a hard edge to their voice as
the muscles tighten under the stress of their anger. Someone
who is sad will have a softer tone, lowered by their loss of

energy due to grief. Already you can recognise how to read a person's immediate frame of mind just from the vibration of their voice. What you now have to do is tune in even further and listen to the unspoken messages within that voice vibration.

Here are some very simple signs to listen for. But remember, you are listening with your higher mind and not just your physical ears. You must be in the alpha state to receive the hidden messages within the vibrations of another person's voice.

1. Stress: This will register in your mind as the tenseness of the speaker's tone triggers the thought.
2. Anger: Rather like stress but the tone is tighter.
3. Lies: Too thoughtful in their responses and uneasy. A light should pop on in your mind when you hear someone telling you lies.
4. Sorrow: Within the voice there will be pauses, little halts and irregular breathing as they fight back the tears.
5. Insincerity: A clever use of words beyond the usual vocabulary of the speaker. They are trying to baffle you, put you off.
6. Happiness: These vibrations are unmistakable. They make you want to bounce along beside them as they almost dance for joy.
7. Depression: Dull vibrations and slow, meandering speech patterns that lose their thread. You cannot mistake the feel of this voice pattern.
8. Ill health: Hope is what you will hear from someone with ill health. They want to be better, and you will feel this within their voice.
9. Desperation: This voice vibration should hit you hard. The speaker will talk very quickly as though time is running out fast. Many questions will be thrown at you – how can I, should I, etc.
10. Confidence: You cannot mistake the tone of a

confident person. They sound measured, balanced and completely in control.

How to Interpret What You Receive

1. Be spontaneous in your response to the individual for whom you are 'reading'.
2. Speak instantly as soon as you receive any insight.
3. Look at any symbols that appear in your mind's eye.

Examples

- A wedding ring: This may mean marriage – or divorce, if it appears broken.
- Flowers: A forthcoming celebration, maybe a birthday.
- A train: A journey to be made.
- An aircraft: A journey overseas.
- The sea: Interpret this by looking at the waves – are they calm or rough?
- Colours: Blue stands for spirituality, red for action.
- Church: A christening or other relevant ceremony.
- Baby: Birth.
- House: Relates to the home.

You have to use your higher consciousness to interpret the symbols you see but you must not try to reason in your mind. Let me give you an example of how *not* to interpret symbols seen through connecting on a voice vibration.

Wrong

You see a house: 'Are you thinking of moving?'
     Never begin a reading with questions. You are there to give what you receive, not fish around for clues. Instead of that line, try to open your consciousness further by saying: 'I

see a house. This is a big (small, detached, etc.) house.' Then tell them what you see and feel. The person you are talking to will respond and you will begin to 'see' more clearly.

Let us look at where the first approach could lead you to:

You see a house: 'Are you thinking of moving?'

Answer: 'No, not that I'm aware of.'

You: 'Well, is someone close to you moving home?'

That way lies trickery. Avoid asking leading questions at all costs. There is no point to them; you prove nothing to the individual seeking your guidance, or to yourself. All you are doing is fooling them and deluding yourself. If that is really the best you can do, then you are not ready to try to 'read' other people. Otherwise you will end up asking people if there is a number 3 on their door and do they live near a corner. In other words, you will become just another phoney, and you must never let that happen to you. It damages you, it hurts the people who seek your help and it is degrading. Believe me, if you do stoop to such dubious practices, those who watch over us in the spirit world will act to stop you. So don't fish for answers with leading questions, just give what you receive and nothing more.

Right

This is how to use the symbols you see properly.

You see a wedding ring: 'I can see a wedding ring, it's a plain band of gold. This is your ring. Do you understand this?'

Answer: 'Yes, I'm married.'

You: 'I see flowers. There is an anniversary soon.'

Answer: 'Yes, it's our wedding anniversary in three weeks' time.'

Now you are tuned in to this individual. You have given what you saw in your mind's eye and interpreted through your higher consciousness. You did not fish for answers, just accepted confirmation. From this point you have an interaction between your higher consciousness, speaking through you, and the individual responding. When the link breaks, as it eventually will, then thank them for trusting you and close down the connection.

The above is a simple example of how to proceed in giving a clairsentient psychic reading to another person using only their voice vibration.

DEALING WITH DESPERATION

With the above in mind, think how you might respond to a person you don't know who comes to you in desperation. Most professional psychics report that the vast majority of first-time clients call to see them because they are desperate for guidance.

This is a very serious matter. You are now walking upon a pathway that could quite quickly place you in a position where strangers see you as being the one who can solve their problems for them. Quite simply, you can't. Nor should you try to do so. Your duty as a psychic person is to give of yourself as you receive, remembering that you are dealing with sensitive human beings.

You must also shun scripts. Never use previously prepared stock phrases. It will happen that you hear someone speaking and you get nothing from the voice whatsoever. It happens to the best psychics at times; it has even happened to me, though not often. In such a case you simply have to admit it. Always stick to the truth. Be aware of your own level of ability and don't pretend to be something that you aren't. You must also be prepared to admit you don't know when asked specific questions that fail to spring an answer into your higher mind. Just say that you are not aware of the answer they are seeking.

Remember that some people are really desperate and you have an absolute duty to them, to yourself and to God not to mislead them.

Clairsentience Assessment Test

This test will enable you to assess your psychic ability to sense things that are unknown to you through your usual five senses. What you are testing here is your heightened sensitivity or clairsentience.

1. Ask a friend to sit with you and explain that you are seeking to test your psychic power of developed sensitivity. They may chuckle a bit but tell them you are serious.
2. Relax and use the breathing techniques you have been practising. Allow yourself to slip gently into the alpha state of altered awareness.
3. Sitting directly opposite your friend, open your mind to them. Have their image on the inner mirror within and think only of them.
4. Without consciously concentrating, or considering the words, speak whatever comes into your mind. Say the words out loud and direct them to your friend. It may be something very simple such as 'You've bought a new pair of shoes' or 'Is your back better today?' Whatever it is, just say it.
5. After approximately five minutes, certainly no more than ten, stop.

Now ask your friend to answer yes to the *one* of the following five statements that they most agree with. Place a tick alongside this statement, then refer to the scoring below.

1. Was the majority of the information I gave you correct?
2. Was some of the information I gave you correct?
3. Was most of the information I gave you wrong?
4. Was all of the information I gave you correct?
5. Was all of the information I gave you wrong?

Scoring

Check the answer given against this list and then check your rating below.
1) 5. 2) 2. 3) −5. 4) 10. 5) −10.

Rating

SCORE 10: Psychic superstar!
SCORE 5: Well done! You are certainly psychic.
SCORE 2: Not too bad for starters.
SCORE −5: Try practising meditation before you have another go.
SCORE −10: Who was your subject, James Randi?

Psychometry

TUNING IN YOUR PSYCHIC POWERS TO INANIMATE OBJECTS

There is a theory that all inanimate objects hold within themselves the residual vibrations of those who have previously had contact with them. By using your psychic powers you can tune in to these vibrations and gain knowledge and information from them concerning those who last had contact with the object. They call this practice psychometry. You can develop this facility by practising tuning yourself in to the hidden vibrations radiating from inanimate objects.

There are three theories as to how psychometry works. The first theory is based on the belief that the vibrations exist as a physical reality and can impart knowledge. Another is that the inanimate object forms a link between the spirit of the previous owner and the individual practising psychometry upon it. This theory suggests that a form of clairvoyance occurs within the higher mind of the person practising psychometry and they tune in to the previous owner's spirit, be that spirit physically alive or in the world beyond. The third theory is that the spirit guide of the person practising psychometry passes the information through mediumship. (We shall be discussing working with spirit guides later in the book.)

My personal belief is that psychometry works because of a mixture of all three of the above theories. As you develop your hidden powers, you will no doubt form your own opinion. In any case, psychometry does work, and below I have designed a simple tutorial to enable you to prove this to yourself and proceed from that point.

Stage 1

1. Take an object, perhaps a ring or watch, that belongs to someone you know very well. This could be your partner.
2. With the owner of this object beside you, hold it gently in your hand.
3. Move your consciousness into the alpha state.
4. Open your third eye by stroking your central forehead in a clockwise direction and 'seeing' your inner eye opening.
5. Now look immediately above the object you are holding and 'see' there images and symbols that pertain to the owner of this object.
6. You know the person this item belongs to, but there will be things that you 'see' which are beyond your conscious knowledge. Speak these out loud and ask for confirmation.
7. Once you have successfully tuned in to an object belonging to your partner or close friend, you will have gained in confidence and can proceed to the next stage.

Stage 2

1. Take an object that belongs, or belonged, to someone you do not know. This object could be a pen, a book or perhaps an item of clothing.
2. As above, switch your consciousness to the alpha state and open your third eye.
3. With the object held gently in your hand, look slightly above it and 'see' symbols and images that relate to the previous owner of this item.
4. In your mind's eye try to picture the person who once owned the object you are now holding.
5. Repeat this practice on a number of items, letting your mind wander freely, though at the same time consciously thinking about who might have previously owned these items.
6. You will begin to develop a kind of sixth sense about inanimate objects if you practise psychometry on a daily basis. Only by repeatedly tuning in to the hidden vibrations of inanimate objects will you become proficient.
7. Test yourself with your friends and their friends.
8. Trust what you receive while practising psychometry. You are developing a unique facility that will, if you believe in your ability, serve you well.

Psychometry Assessment Test

This test will enable you to assess your psychic ability to sense the unseen history of an inanimate object. What you are testing here is your heightened attunement.

1. Ask a friend to bring you an object, perhaps an old watch or a ring, that belongs or used to belong to a close member of their family. This person must be well known to your friend. Ask your friend to avoid direct contact with the object they are bringing as

their own vibrations may interfere with the original vibrations from the actual owner or previous owner.

2. Get your friend to sit opposite you and place the object by your side. Now relax and use the breathing techniques you have been practising. Allow yourself to slip gently into the alpha state of altered awareness.

3. Now take the object in your hands and open your mind to it. Look carefully at this object, hold its image in the mirror of your mind.

4. Without considering what you sense or see, speak the words that come to you. They may be simple things such as 'I see an old lady' or 'There is smoke here'. No matter how odd the images or thoughts are that come to you, say them out loud.

5. After approximately five minutes, certainly no more than ten, stop.

Now ask your friend to answer yes to the *one* of the following five statements that they most agree with. Place a tick alongside this statement, then refer to the scoring below.

1. All of the information I gave was correct and related to the object's owner.

2. Most of the information I gave was incorrect and did not relate to the object's owner.

3. Some of the information I gave was correct and related to the object's owner.

4. All of the information I gave was wrong and did not relate to the object's owner.

5. The majority of the information I gave was right and did relate to the object's owner.

Scoring

Check the answer given against this list, then check your rating below.

1) 10. 2) –5. 3) 2. 4) –10. 5) 5.

Rating

SCORE 10: Psychometer supreme!
SCORE 5: Excellent start, but remember to practise.
SCORE 2: You are clearly sensitive. Keep trying!
SCORE −5: Better luck next time!
SCORE −10: Who owned your object then – the Invisible Man?

Developing Your Hidden Dowsing Ability

The theories about how dowsing works are numerous. One is that the object used as a dowsing instrument is activated by the higher consciousness of the dowser. This is the theory to which I personally subscribe. I believe that our higher self can see and know all things and that by tuning in to this source of boundless knowledge we can discover many things that would be hidden to our physical senses.

I can't in this book examine in detail the history of all the subjects covered, but there is a suggested reading list at the end. For now, we will stick with the above-mentioned theory of how dowsing works. In any case dowsing really does work and, at the end of this tutorial, you will be invited to prove this to yourself.

PENDULUMS

In my experience the best method of dowsing for information is by the use of a pendulum. This may consist of a crystal or some other object suspended at the end of a chain or string. The dowser holds the chain of the pendulum between their thumb and forefinger with the crystal hanging freely approximately 12 to 18 inches below, and asks the pendulum to locate whatever it is they are seeking. This may be water, oil, a lost object or even the answer to a question.

First you must get yourself a pendulum. If need be you can simply suspend a ring on a length of cotton or string. Then you tune your pendulum in to your higher consciousness. I have designed a way to help you to do this.

Tuning Your Pendulum in to Your Higher Consciousness

Note

Do not waste your time trying to swing the pendulum consciously. Such actions will be quite obvious to any observer and you will gain nothing from this whatsoever. Except maybe wrist ache.

---

1. Take a plain sheet of paper and write the words YES and NO upon it in the pattern below:

YES

NO + NO

YES

2. Now suspend the point of the pendulum over the centre of these words and use your previously practised technique to switch into the alpha state.
3. Now say out loud to the pendulum, 'Show me Yes.' You should now see the pendulum swinging upwards and downwards indicating YES.
4. Now say out loud to the pendulum, 'Show me No.' The pendulum should now switch its swing from up and down to left and right indicating NO.

5. Now ask the pendulum a question to which you know the answer. For example 'Is my name X?' You must speak your question out loud. The pendulum should now swing to the correct answer.
6. Try this one more time to assure yourself that the pendulum is giving you the correct answers. You think of a question – perhaps 'Is my head green?' – speak it out loud and note that the pendulum is giving you the correct answer.
7. The pendulum is now tuned in to your higher consciousness and you may go on to the next stage.

There are of course many who doubt that dowsing with a pendulum actually works. Well, dowsing works for me.

Psychologists refer to the *ideomotor effect* to explain the action of the pendulum. This is the effect of subtle muscular movements causing the pendulum to swing. This may very well be so, but I believe that those movements are generated through the higher consciousness of the dowser. This gives the dowser a direct channel to the hidden knowledge that is freely available to the higher self.

Prove the Truth of the Pendulum

Using the above yes/no system, ask your pendulum a series of questions that you do not consciously know the answer to. You will need a friend to help you, or more than one. Tell them you are testing your psychic pendulum – they'll understand, I'm sure!

1. With your mind in the alpha state and the pendulum suspended over the centre of the yes/no box, ask out loud this question: 'Is my friend X married?' When the pendulum swings to the correct answer, you know you are tuned in.
2. Now ask out loud a question about your friend that you do not know the answer to. For example, 'Is my

friend X colour blind?' Check the answer the pendulum gives you with your friend. You will now know that the pendulum is indeed telling you the truth.

3. Next, ask a more obscure question. The answer always has to be able to be given as a direct yes or no. For example, ask out loud, 'Are my friend X's mother's eyes blue?' You will be surprised to discover that the pendulum knows the right answer to even such an improbable question.

4. Next, try getting your friend to ask questions that they know the answer to but you do not. You simply repeat the question out loud and watch as the pendulum swings to the right answer.

You should now be absolutely convinced that you are able to dowse the truth through your pendulum. You can do it, I know you can! All you need is total faith in yourself and the ability to move your consciousness into the alpha state.

From this point on, proceed as you see fit. But remember, no really silly questions that might scare you or hurt anyone else. Be a true and honest instrument and you will receive the answers you seek.

Dowsing for Lost Articles

Once you have mastered the art of tuning in your pendulum, there are many uses to which you can put it. You can find missing or lost objects through your newly discovered ability as a dowser. All you have to do to locate a lost item is to:

1. Hold an image of it in your mind.
2. Go to the area where you think it might be.
3. Tune in your pendulum with your mind in the alpha state.
4. Ask the pendulum out loud to show you where the missing item is.

5. Follow the swing of your pendulum, no matter how unlikely this might seem.
6. Look in the area indicated.

Once you have proved this to yourself a few times by locating things like lost keys or library books, you will be confident in your ability. So put it to the test!

Dowsing Assessment Test

This test will enable you to assess your psychic power to locate hidden or lost objects by the use of a pendulum tuned in to your higher self.

1. Ask a friend to help you with this test. You need a reasonably large open area, such as a garden, and also an object belonging to yourself. This object could be a watch or a ring.
2. Hand the object to your friend and ask them to hide the object out of your sight in the area you have chosen. They should note very carefully the exact location.
3. With the object now hidden in the open area, take your pendulum and tune it in to yourself by the usual method; show me Yes, show me No. Now picture the object you are seeking in your mind and ask the pendulum to show you where it is. You should speak the words out loud; say 'Pendulum, show me where my watch [or whatever] is.'
4. The pendulum should transmit a very slight tug or pull in the general direction of the object you are seeking. At all times during the test you must keep the image of the object you are seeking in your mind. Keep speaking the words 'Show me where it is' out loud and follow the pull of the pendulum.
5. When you arrive at the spot where your friend has hidden the object, the pendulum should swing very

powerfully. Allow yourself to be guided by the pendulum, no matter how unlikely the area you are taken to might seem.

Obviously, if you found the hidden object, you proved to yourself that dowsing does actually work. However, if you failed to find the object, do not despair. Dowsing requires considerable practise.

Now read these following statements and place a tick alongside the *one* that you most agree with.

1. The pendulum led me to within a few feet of the hidden object.
2. The pendulum did nothing, it just hung there all limp.
3. The pendulum led me directly to the hidden object and I found it.
4. The pendulum led me all over the place and we found nothing.
5. The pendulum eventually led me to the right area, where I chanced to find the object.

Scoring

Check the selected statement against this list and then refer to the assessment chart below.
1) 2. 2) –10. 3) 10. 4) –5. 5) 5.

Rating

SCORE 10: Dowser's delight!
SCORE 5: Very good level of attunement.
SCORE 2: Keep trying!
SCORE –5: Nice walk?
SCORE –10: Dowsing dunce.

Telepathy

In the above sections we have looked at ways of tuning your mind and higher consciousness in to other people on a level of vibration. Telepathy is one stage further along the process of personal attunement. This involves the passing of information between two people without recourse to the accepted five senses.

Below is a simple test that you can use to assess your ability. You may also use this test to actually develop your psychic telepathic power. Tests such as the one below are undertaken in parapsychology laboratories throughout the world. They are perfectly harmless and lots of fun. Good luck!

TESTING AND DEVELOPING YOUR TELEPATHIC POWERS

This test will enable you to discover whether you have the psychic ability to receive and/or transmit images to another person through telepathy. Used regularly, it will enable you to develop and log your progress. Only by practise can you proceed to the higher levels of raised consciousness and psychic ability.

Ask the person you are closest to in life to assist you in the test. If they won't – maybe they think you've taken leave of your senses – then ask a friend. Tell them you are testing your psychic powers and want to conduct a scientific experiment using a form of Zener cards. That should do the trick.

Here are five symbols for you to copy onto five separate, identical sheets of blank card or paper:

1. You require two separate rooms with a chair and a table in each.
2. Place the five sheets of paper with the symbols on them on the table where you will sit.
3. Place a blank sheet of paper with a pencil or pen on the table in the other room where your partner in this experiment will sit.
4. Show your partner the five symbols.
5. Now take your partner into their room and sit them down at their table. Explain that you will be transmitting the image of just one of the five shapes to

their mind. They should relax. When an image pops into their mind, they should draw it on the blank sheet of paper.

6. With your partner now seated in the other room, sit at the table in your room and turn the five symbols face down to the table. Now close your eyes and shuffle these, finally selecting just one.

7. Open your eyes and look at the symbol you have selected. Picture this image clearly in your mind. You must see it perfectly both on the table before you and within your mind's eye.

8. Now send this image to your partner. Think of them. Speak their name out loud. Imagine the image of the symbol before you flying through the walls into their mind. Continue doing this for two to three minutes.

9. Go into the room where your partner is and see what they have drawn.

10. Repeat steps 6 to 9 five times. Each time make a note of the image you sent and attach to this the picture your partner drew.

11. Now reverse the roles. As your partner attempts to send the images to you, as in steps 6 to 9 above, you just relax and make your mind receptive.

12. Now see how many you got right.

TELEPATHY ASSESSMENT

Transmitting

Correct:

5/5 Amazing! You are not only telepathic, you are super-telepathic, but then you knew I was going to say that, didn't you?

4/5 Incredible! This is a brilliant result.

3/5 Wonderful! You are a telepathic star transmitter.

2/5 Double the average score. Very good, keep practising.

1/5 This is what you'd get right just by guessing.
0/5 Why worry? You can always shout.

Receiving

Correct:
5/5 Astounding! You should be a professional card player.
4/5 Remarkable! No doubt about it, you are telepathic plus.
3/5 Great stuff! This is triple the average score.
2/5 Better than the average – well done! Practise.
1/5 Average, but don't give up! Keep trying.
0/5 Well, telepathy is perhaps not your main psychic gift.

How to Foretell
Your Own Future

Foretelling the future is quite simple. In fact, anyone can do it. The difficult bit is getting it right! In my work as a psychic medium, I'm frequently consulted by people who want to know what lies before them in years to come. I can, and indeed often do, see and hear details concerning major events that await those who ask me to look into the future for them. However, with knowledge and practise, individuals can foretell their own futures. There are many books published on a wide range of predictive techniques, from astrology to tarot and all points between. In this chapter I will discuss very briefly my personal beliefs on how and why we can enable ourselves to foresee the future.

First let me state that I believe that the future already exists and is known to our higher selves. Look at the illustration on page 132 as an example of life in linear terms as we usually perceive it. Think how this relates to your life.

Imagine that you are in the vehicle and are driving through time. Each mile is a year of your life. You have set the mileage at zero when you began. Now, look at the reading and think back in time through all those years (miles). One mile ago is clear in your mind. You have a picture of all the

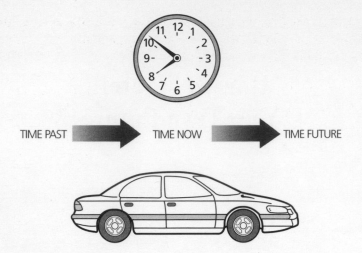

places you have just passed and the people you met. But if you go back fifteen miles, the memory is less distinct, though the images are there, you can remember.

Now think how you arrived at your present position. Had you turned a different corner, you would not now be where you are. Think of the future then as being the product of the past. It exists because of what has already been. You have created your future by the decisions you made both before you began and during this journey that is your physical life in this material world.

While physically alive, you have free will at all times and the freedom to make choices. This life is a learning process and you are given the opportunity to make decisions. However, make the wrong decisions and you will have to repeat mistakes made in previous incarnations. The idea is to get your life right and learn what you need to learn to progress spiritually. To know what lies ahead of you, look within yourself. The answer to your future destiny is there on the map you drew before you set out on this great adventure. Foretelling the future reveals the potential, but only you can make it reality by your actions. Thoughts and promises count for nothing. By your deeds you are known.

Next, consider the illustration (below) of life as a cycle of interlinked events. This is your physical life seen at the NOW point in nonlinear terms.

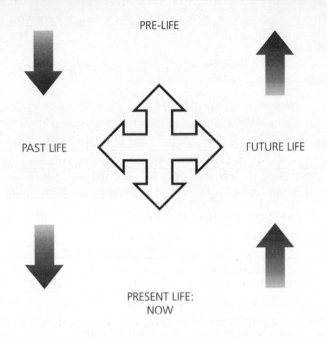

PRE-LIFE

PAST LIFE   FUTURE LIFE

PRESENT LIFE:
NOW

Pre-Life

This is the period between physical death and physical birth. During this pre-life period the soul is in the spirit world preparing itself for a future incarnation. This episode in your eternal life is hidden from your consciousness.

Past Life

This period in your physical life has already passed. You will have conscious memory of events that have occurred during this part of your physical life. These events, and also previous past-life events, have shaped your present. Your previous incarnations are a part of this very important area of your eternal life.

Present Life: Now

This is you as you are today. You have knowledge of your immediate previous life and your hopes and aspirations for the future. You know who you are now and where you came from in this physical life.

Future Life

This is the period of your life, both eternal and physical, that is before you. What lies ahead is directly linked to what lies in the past. This future life can be glimpsed through reference to your higher all-knowing self. Before you set forth on this journey of life, you knew your destination. Only you, the real you, knows whether you have followed the map you drew in the world beyond long before you were born.

In foretelling the future you are seeking access to hidden knowledge. That is to say that the information exists but you, in your physical body, cannot comprehend it. However, there are methods whereby you can bypass the limitations imposed upon you by your physical form. The key to the hidden door to your future lies within your grasp.

YOU IN RELATION TO THE FUTURE

The illustration on the next page shows you in relation to the past, the present or material world, the future and the world of spirit. Note that you are grounded in the material world. This to you in your physical body is the tangible reality of now. Note also that the recent past touches you; it has helped to form the now that you are experiencing.

The near and distant future are not consciously seen or known to you in your physical form. But your higher self has access to the hidden knowledge that is the truth of your future life.

To foretell the future, you must move your consciousness from the material plane to your higher self. Only then will you gain access to the hidden truth.

Foretelling the Future II: Divination

Before undertaking any form of personal divination, you must shift your consciousness into the alpha state. You will by now have developed your own knack of entering the alpha state, maybe through controlled breathing, as I do, or through linking to an inanimate object, and letting go.

ASKING FOR GUIDANCE

What you are about to do is ask for guidance from, or through, your higher consciousness. Your conscious mind must not even be allowed to consider anything that is given to you during this exercise. You will simply accept the visions you see and the messages you receive. These are for contemplation once you have completed this simple and very relaxing interaction with your higher mind.

Setting the Question

You will decide upon the specific question that you require the answer to some time before you begin to seek guidance.

This may be something simple, such as asking if you should join a bridge club or become a member elsewhere. There may be more pressing problems that require life-changing decisions to be made. Whatever your question is, write it down.

Having written down your question, you must now hold it in your mind as you prepare to enter the alpha state of altered consciousness. While in the alpha state, you may seek guidance using one of the following simple techniques.

CHANNELLED RECORDED VOICE GUIDANCE (CRVG)

Equipment

- A cassette or reel-to-reel audiotape recorder with a microphone
- A new blank audiotape
- A pad of plain paper
- A pen or pencil

This form of personal divination is best conducted by the questioner sitting on their own. Select a quiet room that is warm and comfortable and where there will be no disturbances. Set aside thirty minutes for this and agree with a third party to call you at a specific time. You should ensure that there is someone else in the house when you undertake this. It is perfectly safe, but you just might fall asleep.

Step-by-Step CRVG

1. Take the tape recorder and fit in a blank, unused tape.
2. Place this in a position close to where you intend to sit during the CRVG.
3. Switch the tape recorder to Record and ensure that the microphone is pointing in your direction.

4. Use your personal technique to enter the alpha state.

5. Once in your altered state of consciousness, speak freely and without thought or consideration for what you are saying. You must let the words flow through you. You are not thinking about these words. These words do not come from your logical mind, they are from your higher mind. Do not even try to understand what you are saying.

6. Having spoken out loud for a period of no more than ten minutes, stop speaking and relax. You should practise the breathing exercises you have mastered and gradually bring yourself out of the alpha state.

7. Now rewind the tape recorder to the beginning of your CRVG session and press Play. You should have a note pad and pencil with you to make notes. Listen carefully to your recorded voice and try to interpret the words spoken. Within these words you may find the answer to your question.

You may repeat this exercise in personal divination daily. Keep records of the questions you ask and the answers you receive. Given time, practise and total honesty, you will quickly become able to channel through your higher consciousness. In time this may develop and you may find yourself receiving direct communication from you spirit guides. At that point you really are developing the hidden potential within yourself and you may wish to seek further guidance. This I earnestly and highly recommend. Please read the chapter dealing with further development, and be aware that we all, at some time in our progression, need to stop and assess where we are going.

Automatic Writing

Equipment

- A pad of plain paper
- A pen or pencil

This form of personal divination involves the questioner sitting at a table or desk with a familiar pen and a pad of plain paper. The chair you sit in must be comfortable and the table clear of clutter and objects that may distract you. Try to sit alone and away from the general everyday noise. The object is to let your hand write or draw whatever the spirits wish to express. You are not the master of this work, you are simply the instrument through which the message is being passed.

This exercise should take no more than thirty minutes, so tell whoever else is in your home to call you in half an hour. As previously, use your own personal technique to enter the alpha state.

Step-by-Step Automatic Writing

1. Take the pen or pencil in your hand and hold it very loosely. Do not grip it tightly as you normally might. Let it rest gently between your thumb and forefinger.
2. Place the pen or pencil lightly upon the top sheet of the pad of plain paper.
3. Letting go of all conscious thought, let the pen move freely across the paper. You may feel a gentle tingling sensation in your hand as the point of the pen begins to move.
4. Watch as the pen or pencil writes. You may feel the words forming in your mind but don't attempt to create them consciously on the page. The pen or pencil will automatically transfer the words you see in your mind's eye onto the paper.

5. Don't attempt to read ahead of the written words or even guess what images are being drawn.

6. If the pen or pencil scribbles and runs about the page, then speak out loud, saying, 'Take control and write slowly.' You are now communicating and as the medium for this communication you must become a good instrument.

7. Don't be concerned if this first attempt fails to produce anything that could remotely be considered as automatic writing. After twenty minutes at the most, stop and try to decipher what may or may not have been written.

8. In trying to decipher the meaning within the words and images that have been created, look first of all for simple explanations and basic words such as 'love' and 'house', especially if they hold specific meaning for you at this time. The writing may contain predictions; for example, it might say 'move house August'. Note these in your diary for future reference.

9. Keep records of your automatic writing sessions so that you can refer back to these. For example, if in a session of automatic writing the pen or pencil made a prediction and you had noted it in your diary, then when it happens, you have proof.

10. Don't allow yourself to become a slave to automatic writing. You should set aside a specific period, perhaps twice a week, to undertake this. More than this is excessive and the results will certainly deteriorate.

The gift of communication through automatic writing is not given to everyone. And only by honest and open perseverance will you be able to develop this gift if it has been given to you. One early indication is the tingling sensation in the hand holding the pen. Another is the sense that words are being whispered in your mind or appear as visions on your inner eye. If this gift is yours, then you are indeed blessed. Treat it with great respect for you have been chosen to accept guidance from the higher realms.

A note of caution: if the communications you receive contain negative messages, you must question these. Your higher consciousness will not give you disconcerting information, nor would any evolved spirit guide.

You are personally responsible for interpreting what you receive through automatic writing, or indeed any other channel of communication. When doing so, the onus is upon you to do it with love, hope and a charitable disposition.

CARTOMANCY: DIVINATION USING CARDS

The practice of divination using cards, dice or dominoes is generically termed cartomancy. I use no such devices, but there is a place for these within the realm of psychic development. The power to divine the future lies within individuals and not within inanimate objects such as playing cards. I believe that those who use such divination devices are really manipulating them as a tool to access their personal alpha state. There is nothing essentially wrong with this practice and, for some, card decks and particularly Tarot decks form part of the key to their ability to foretell.

DIVINATION BY TAROT CARDS

Many professional psychics use divination tools to enable them to 'see' the future for their clients. In this section I will discuss the ways in which these work and how you can get the best results from them.

The origin of Tarot cards dates back to before the birth of Christ. They are probably the most popular of all divination tools and have become a byword for fortune telling. Many clients expect psychics to use cards. I never do, but you can, and this is how to make them work for you.

The Tarot deck is divided into two sections, the Major Arcana of 22 symbols, or picture cards, and the Minor Arcana of 56 cards subdivided into four suits: Swords, Clubs, Cups and Coins. Study these cards and form a picture of them in your mind. Look at the Major Arcana and consider the pictures on them. Your deck should have a booklet outlining the meaning of each card. Read this and try to remember the meanings, at least of the Major Arcana.

Let me give you a very simple example of how to construct a psychic reading by interpreting selected cards from the 22 Major Arcana of a Tarot deck:

1. Shuffle the 22 cards of the Major Arcana while asking a simple question in your mind.
2. When you are satisfied with the shuffle, stop.
3. Now deal five cards face down in a vertical line in front of you, starting at the bottom.
4. Read these in the order you dealt them, as follows:

Distant Future

This card indicates what awaits the questioner in the years ahead. This card is before the questioner.

Immediate Future

This card confronts the questioner in the period immediately before them. In time, this card indicates weeks and months.

Now

This card relates to the questioner's position as it is now at this precise moment in time. It identifies the questioner in relation to all other matters.

Recent Past

This card shows the questioner the situation that has immediately passed or is passing. It is behind the questioner and will relate directly to the Now situation.

Distant Past

This card refers to the questioner's previous years. It is the foundation upon which the future has been built.

Interpretation

Assuming you've boned up on it, you will understand the meaning of each of the five cards displayed. Now switch into the alpha state and speak.

If you are giving this reading for another person, you must remember to treat their feelings with the utmost respect. For example, if the Immediate Future is showing the thirteenth card of the Major Arcana, which often features a skull and means change or death of the old self, be tactful. Do not say anything drastic like 'You'll be dead within a month.' You may say 'Major changes right in front of you' and then consider whether the questioner is about to move house or job. Predicting physical death should *never* be a part of your reading.

Practise reading the Tarot deck using the different card spreads outlined in their accompanying booklet. Try to discover the spread that works best for you. There are many books on the subject of the Tarot and a suggested reading list is to be found at the end of this book.

The most important part of using the Tarot is your higher consciousness. Only you can interpret your cards and you must make them *your* cards. You do this by keeping them in a black cloth pouch and placing this beneath your pillow on your bed. These cards are your cards and no one else should be allowed to use them to read with.

Immediately before a reading, clear your mind and try to enter the alpha state. You can do this by using the breathing techniques discussed in the chapter on meditation. As you read with the cards, try to 'see' the future. It is there slightly above the cards as they lie on the table before you. Images should appear in your mind's eye, thoughts will flow and words form themselves; you must now speak these aloud. Be confident. Be relaxed. Tell the questioner what you see. Tarot works through you, not through cards; they are divination tools, you are the psychic, and you 'see' the future.

With the Tarot, practise improves your ability. Study your cards, use every opportunity to read with them. Make them a part of yourself and you will soon discover that you are indeed psychic, as we all are. The Tarot is one way to discover your personal ability to 'see' the future for yourself and, perhaps, for others.

DIVINATION USING PLAYING CARDS

Like the Tarot deck, the playing cards form only a part of the key to enable you to 'see' the future for yourself and others. There are many books on the subject of card reading and there is a suggested list at the end of this book. Here is a simple example of how to use an ordinary pack of 52 playing cards to enable you to foretell the future for yourself or another person.

The Meaning of the Four Suits

Hearts: Love affairs. Marriage. Domestic matters. Friendships.
Clubs: Money. Financial affairs. Material possessions.
Diamonds: Employment. Travel. Business affairs. New ventures.
Spades: Difficulties. Sadness. Ill fortune. Misadventure.

The Meaning of the Main Cards

Aces
Hearts: Joy and happiness.
Clubs: Good luck with money.
Diamonds: Business or work correspondence.
Spades: Legal matters.

Kings
Hearts: A fair-haired man.
Clubs: A dark-haired man.
Diamonds: A powerful person.
Spades: A judge or police officer.

Queens
Hearts: A fair woman who is very kind.
Clubs: A dark woman.
Diamonds: A fair-haired but mean woman.
Spades: A divorced lady.

Jacks
Hearts: A young man intending love.
Clubs: A dark man, a lover.
Diamonds: A man in uniform.
Spades: A handsome dark-haired man.

Interpretation

As with the Tarot cards, you must find the spread that best answers your questions. Here is a very simple example of how to use ordinary playing cards to foretell your own or another person's future.

Take the full deck of 52 playing cards and shuffle these until you feel it right to stop. Beginning with the top card, deal out a horizontal line of ten cards starting at your left. They refer to the questioner's time scheme in pairs:

1.	2.	3.	4.	5.	6.	7.	8.	9.	10.
Distant		Recent		The		Immediate		Distant	
past		past		present		future		future	

With knowledge of the main picture cards and the basic
meaning of the four suits, you should now be able to give
yourself or another person a psychic reading by interpreting
this spread. The four suits are a basic guide. For example, if
Hearts are the predominant suit, then you 'see' love affairs.
If Clubs are predominant, money is highlighted. However,
you must never interpret any spread of cards to mean that
yourself or any other person is about to suffer some horrible
misfortune. Be sensible about what you say and bear in mind
that you are using cards as a tool to unlock your inert psychic
powers. The object is to link in with your higher consciousness, not to play at being Madame Arcate.

PART 3

THE SPIRITUAL DIMENSION

Introduction

Welcome to the part of this book that is closest to my heart. I am a spirit medium and throughout my life I have experienced the pure wonderment of communication with spirits alive in the world beyond. Within the following pages you will read of the incredible insights that I have been given. I am not trying to convert you to some outrageous esoteric belief system. I don't expect you to abandon your personal position with regard to your religious or agnostic understanding of life. What I hope you will gain from reading the spiritual dimension of my book is a better insight into what I believe. You are free to take whatever you like from what follows. If you do not agree with me, I don't mind. I offer my insights to you in the hope and trust that you will read them with love in your heart. Please be assured that I wrote them with love and compassion in my own heart.

If, having read this section, you feel you would like to learn more about the spiritual dimension, or psychic world, then there are a number of ways in which you can proceed. What I would caution you against is getting involved with charlatans and false prophets. Be very circumspect in all your dealings with those who profess to have the ability to communicate with those alive in the world of spirit. There are many frauds out there and it can be difficult to discern between the pretender and the honest medium. There is no certain foolproof way to ensure you are not hoodwinked, but if you ever hear a so-called medium say 'Is there a number 3 on your door?' – run!

A Spiritualist church is perhaps the ideal place for you to seek advice about visiting a medium or to advance your search for the truth of eternal life. Spiritualism is a type of Christianity. You may find such churches throughout the Western world and many feature very good spirit mediums who will be pleased to offer you help and advice.

I would not recommend that you begin your further development by joining any commercial group that requires you to pay money without checking them out first with your local Spiritualist church. It is an unfortunate fact that some unscrupulous people use the field of psychic studies simply to further their own material ends. There is also a real risk that you could encounter pseudo-Satanists. These are dangerous not because they are agents of some mythological demon, but because their sworn intent is to exploit you. So if you ever get invited to dance in a moon-suit around some stone altar in the middle of the night, decline at once. Not only is it pointless, it is likely to be very cold too.

Remember you are a child of God, born with free will and with a duty to your own self. If you find within this section of my book some few words that bring you closer to your own truth, then my work has been done properly.

Mediumship

In the previous chapters you have read how to meditate, enter the alpha state, open your third eye, develop and practise clairsentience and even try divination, among other things. But mediumship is different from anything you have so far attempted in this book. Mediumship, in its truest sense, is the communication between those alive in the world of spirit and those living in this material world. Mediumship in relation to psychic ability is what a lion is to a lamb. They may be in the same field but one is far more powerful than the other.

I receive direct messages from the world beyond through my spirit guide Sam. I have worked with my guide all my human life and I trust what he tells me absolutely. Sam gives me insights into the future, he speaks to me of things to come, and experience tells me that he is right. When I sit as a medium for other people, Sam brings their guides, friends and family to me from the next world. Sometimes I 'see' these visiting spirits within my mind. On occasions I have watched as these spirits materialise in front of me. I hear the messages they bring for those they love who are sitting with me. My guide helps them to communicate through me and I receive these messages in various ways within my mind. Sam will even pass on the messages himself if the visiting spirit finds it too difficult. Mediumship is, quite simply, a most beautiful and God-given gift. And being a gift it cannot, with any hope of success, be taught. You either are a medium or you are not. It's as simple as that.

However, there may be those among the readers of this book who have mediumistic powers but have failed, so far, to recognise these. Look at the check list below and assess your potential to be a medium for the spirit world. Just read through the list and – honestly – place a tick alongside any statement that you feel matches your personal experiences. When you have done this, refer to the assessment chart and follow the advice that pertains to your level of experience and potential.

Don't be disappointed if you discover that you are not really a gifted medium. I wanted to be a world-famous foot-baller once upon a time, but I never really made the top notch. You see, I was a medium playing football. Perhaps you have another gift all of your own. I know we are all special in God's eyes. So be happy with your talents and use them as you were intended to use them, without fear and with hope and love in your heart.

Are You a Spirit Medium?

Read through the following statements, placing a tick along-side any that you can truthfully say pertain to you. Then total all your ticks, counting each as one, and refer to the assessment chart at the end.

> **Note**
>
> The key word in this assessment is *frequently*. In the previous test of your psychic potential we were looking at infrequent paranormal occurrences.

1. Are you frequently visited by unseen entities when you are in bed at night?
2. Do you frequently respond to voices calling your name, only to discover that there is nobody present?
3. Do you frequently hear a voice in your mind speaking to you of matters beyond your conscious understanding?
4. Has any full-time professional spirit medium ever told you that you are a developing medium?
5. Were any of your parents or grandparents recognised as a medium?
6. Have you ever looked at another human being and seen a light shining around them like an aura?
7. Have you frequently observed paranormal activity around you, such as doors opening on their own or taps turning themselves on?
8. During the hours of darkness, have you ever woken and seen your bedroom flooded with a milky white, slightly luminous mist?
9. Do you frequently experience the sensation of being touched by unseen hands that are distinctly cold?
10. When you go into a Spiritualist church, does the spirit medium usually approach you with a message concerning your mediumship?

Assessing Your Personal Potential to be a Spirit Medium

Total

8–10: You should seek advice immediately from your local Spiritualist church. Go to the minister, explain what you are experiencing and ask them for guidance. It is most unwise to proceed to develop as a spirit medium on your own. If you have answered the above truthfully and with love in your heart, then go to your nearest Spiritualist church and tell them Derek Acorah sent you. In the meantime, refer *now* to the chapter in this book titled 'Self-Protection'. Read this and then close down your channels. Do this with hope and love in your heart. You are not shutting out your spirit friends; what you are doing is preparing a better pathway for them as you develop your mediumship in a safe and controlled environment.

5–7: If you have been absolutely truthful in answering the above and have no doubt in your mind that these things are happening to you, then you are developing the gift of mediumship. Do not play at this development; it is a serious matter and you should seek out your local Spiritualist church for advice. The minister there will tell you of local development circles where you can allow your gift to progress in safety. It is not safe to try and communicate with the world beyond on your own while you are developing. They may contact you, but if you open your channels, anyone from the next world could drop in. Once you have been taught how to control your mediumship and work with your spirit guide, you will be communicating effectively and safely. In the meantime, refer to the chapter in the book titled 'Self-Protection'. Read this and then close down your channels. You will soon be able to open them again when you sit in the Spiritualist development circle.

1–4: Any of the above experiences is a firm indication that you have a certain degree of gift as a potential spirit medium. The development of this gift should only take place under the guidance of an established medium. If you are serious about your development go to your local Spiritualist church and ask the minister to direct you to a development circle. In the meantime, if the phenomena you experience cause you alarm, refer to the chapter in this book titled 'Self-Protection'. Read this and then close down your channels.

0: So what are you gifts? Playing football? Bridge? Writing? We all have our own abilities and yours are clearly not as a medium. Worry not, just get on and enjoy developing the gifts God did give you.

The Joy of Being a Spirit Medium

All my life I have been able to receive communication from the world of spirit. My very first message to another person was given to my own granny in her house in Bootle where we were living. I was just six years old at the time and had been playing with my toy soldiers on the landing upstairs. The rest of the family, including Gran, were downstairs. Mum was making the evening meal. I clearly recall hearing her call me down; 'Come on and get your tea, our Derek!' she yelled. I didn't want to go down and leave my soldiers. Then suddenly I felt a hand ruffling my hair. It was a friendly action, like adults do to children. Looking up, I saw an old man's happy face smiling at me. 'Come here, you young scamp,' he said and playfully patted my head. 'Tell your gran that it's great here, I'm having fun and love her lots.'

I said I would, turned and ran down the stairs to the kitchen where everyone else was already eating.

Over the sago pudding I recalled the old man I had met upstairs and passed his message to Gran. She went very still. 'Can you describe this man?' she asked.

Well, I tried; 'Bigger than me, grey hair, happy face' – not much use, I expect, thinking back.

Then Gran went to her old oak cupboard and lifted off a photograph of herself and a man. It was him! 'That's your grandfather,' she said. 'He died five years before you were born.'

I will never forget that late afternoon after I had met the man who wasn't there at the top of the stairs. My gran showed me many more pictures of her late husband, my grandfather, and we laughed as she told us funny stories about him and his favourite dog that used to pee in the house. Then Gran took me in her arms and told me I was a very, very special little boy and I had brought her a lot of joy that day. I will never, ever forget that first glorious experience of bringing hope and love to my gran.

For me, the following poem captures the way it must feel

to be a spirit seeking to communicate their undying love to someone they had to leave behind.

I Was Gone

by
JOHN G. SUTTON

I was gone this morning
When I looked in the mirror
To comb my hair
In the living room I searched
There was no one in my chair

I was gone this afternoon
When I tried to dry your tears
It's so hard
To see you crying
For those long ago years

I was gone this evening
As you went to climb the stair
Then you turned
But didn't see me
My footsteps trod the air

I was gone in the moonlight
As the silent silver shone
Then I heard you whisper
My name
But I was gone.

As a spirit medium I can act as a bridge between this world and the next. You see, not only do we who are physically alive seek to communicate, those living in the spirit world seek to do so as well. There is great joy to be gained from being a true and honest medium who helps to bring both sides of the great divide together. If this is to be your chosen path, then tread it with care. You must show understanding and compassion for all those you meet along the way, be they incarnate or discarnate. Your duty is to respect them as the children of God that they most surely are.

The Psychic World

Beyond this material plane that in our waking state we perceive as reality lies the psychic world. This is the world of our immortal soul. Since time immemorial, humankind has sought to understand what awaits us in the next dimension. As Shakespeare wrote, 'In that sleep of death, what dreams may come?' My personal explanation comes from the insights and visions I have been granted by my spirit guides.

THE PHYSICAL WORLD

Our bodies are the physical shells in which we as spirits are incarnated. We are not here by accident, we have chosen to be born before we enter this world. With free will we pre-selected our parents and our physical body. We were alive long before we were incarnated in flesh and bone as we are today. Then we lived in the dimension beyond this material plane with our spiritual brothers and sisters. Those around us that we see as fellow human beings are people we have known before as members of our 'soul group'. Together we are evolving, moving ever closer to our ultimate divine destiny. Not one of us, not even the most evil among us, will eventually fail. Although it might take ten thousand physical lifetimes, or more, we are all destined to arrive in the light of God's highest kingdom.

In my father's house this physical world is the lowest land. It is an often dark, yet glorious creation. We are incarnated here to learn certain spiritual lessons. And learn these we must. It is pointless to try to avoid the inevitable progression. You will learn what you need to learn in this lifetime or a later one. You will learn and you will progress. There is no death so, no matter how long it takes, you are going to become one with God.

If you seek to know about hell, look around you. We create our own hell and we create our own pathway to heaven. The choice is yours. And as you can see by observing your surroundings, your choice clearly lacks something. That something is called spiritual understanding and you can find it only within your own soul. For God is within you and you are one of his children.

WHY DO SO MANY SUFFER IN THIS WORLD?

We all select our own personal pathway before we are born and some of us have selected difficult pathways. This is to enable the evolving soul to make progress in this physical lifetime. It is for us to be strong in our faith that everything in this world is for a purpose. We must understand that our pain is transient.

There are those among us who have chosen to walk a hard road. They have a karmic duty to fulfil and though they cry now, in the ultimate light of understanding their tears shall purify them.

Physical suffering is piteous to see, especially in young children, but spiritual progression cannot be achieved by simply surviving. The soul within our physical form has to develop and there are karmic influences, checks and balances. For each negative aspect there is a positive aspect. The only way to understand this is by personal experience. For we could not know the light without first knowing the darkness.

INSTANT KARMA

As we walk through our earthly lives in our physical bodies, we are accruing karma, be it good or bad. For some, the deeds they do will be so serious that the karmic influences they create will be recorded and credited or debited to their eternal account in the world beyond. However, minor hurts and less important acts of goodness may receive instant karmic results. Let me give you an example from my own less than perfect life.

I was scheduled to fly to Spain for a business meeting. I had my ticket, I had booked the taxi, I was all set. Then, the day before, my mother telephoned me and asked me to speak to my older brother who needed advice. Well, in my arrogance, I said no. He had previously mocked my mediumship and now, I thought, he dared to ask *me* for help. The next day I got to the airport to find that my flight was delayed over thirteen hours. When I eventually went to check in at the airline desk, they told me my ticket was invalid. I couldn't go. Instant karma!

The next morning I telephoned my brother and gave him all the help I possibly could. I recognised my mistake. I had become self-important, a little too sure of myself, and my karmic balance was in deficit. So I got a lesson. Now I know that when I'm wrong, things happen that I don't like. I am being very gently guided towards the right path. It's rather like taking a wrong turning in the woods and bumping into a tree.

WHY ARE THERE ACTS OF CRIME AND VIOLENCE?

Goodness and evil are opposite sides of the human personality. Yet our thoughts on good and bad are not fixed, immutable points of cosmic law. Our physical lives are subject to the rules of the society in which we live. And the manmade rules or laws which surround us help to formulate our thoughts. That which we today think to be evil, for example burning people at the stake, was once thought to be right and proper. Indeed, mutilation, torture and death are still meted out in some countries by those professing devout religious beliefs. Our personal values are subject to the socialisation process we experience within our present earthly lives. Were we to travel back in time to the Middle Ages, we would doubtless be horrified by the accepted practices of that era. So you see that our perception of what constitutes crime and violence shifts through the ages. In war we award medals to killers. In peacetime the very same deeds would result in imprisonment. In truth, we are all learning our lessons and slowly evolving towards the light of God's eternal love. If we did not know evil, we could never recognise good.

Of course we all think we know the difference between good and evil, but in the eye of time, are we right? Ask yourself this question as the test: Do I feel that what I am doing or about to do will harm or needlessly hurt another living entity? If the answer is yes, then whatever it is you are doing or about to do is evil. Do it and you will incur a degree of karmic debt commensurate with your actions. This debt must be repaid; there is no escape. Time may pass, a thousand lifetimes come and go, but eventually you will redress the balance. You cannot progress spiritually until you have done so and there is no escape from your duty. There is no death.

ENTERING THE NEXT WORLD

It is the most natural thing to physically die and the one
certainty in this earthly life. I write not of accidental death or
violent death but of the predetermined physical death of our
corporeal bodies. Death is but a sleep and an awakening. We
close our eyes and wake to another dawn in the world beyond
the confines of this heavy land. Imagine a world without pain
and suffering where we are that which we are! The next
world is such a place and we prepare our future homes with
every deed and thought of our daily lives.

There will be those who have built themselves a paradise
in the world beyond. Yet there are others who must face the
foulness of their wasted lives. But as there is no death, only
eternal life, for those whose recent incarnation was a negative
journey, there is always tomorrow and tomorrow and tomorrow. However, that tomorrow must and will contain karmic
reparation; the scales have to balance. So the next incarnation of a soul in serious karmic deficit could prove to be
difficult indeed.

BETWEEN TWO WORLDS

Passing over from this material world to the next is, in the
usual way, without trauma. The soul recognises that it has
left the body and is still alive. Sometimes the soul or spirit
refuses to leave the earthly realms where it lived while incarnated in a physical body. When this occurs, the spirit can
become trapped between this world and the next. In such
cases we have a ghost, in the truest sense of the term. This
ghost will be similar in both looks and attitude to the person
that it once physically was. So if this was a big, angry, igno-
rant man, then you have a troublesome phantom that may
refuse to accept that it is without form.

For most of us the transition between physical life and life
in the spirit world will be rather like a short journey. We may

be met by those we loved who have passed to spirit before us. When this occurs, we come to realise that we are beyond our bodies. This will be a joyous experience and one that should be full of love. Others may find themselves at a railway station or an airport waiting to catch a train or a plane to an uncertain destination. This is a cultural matter, and someone whose earthly life has been spent somewhere like Lapland will probably experience transition by sledge. The whole process of journeying between the material and the spirit world is created to enable the departing soul to feel at ease. There is no fear between this world and the next. Everything is calm and the timetables are always correct, even the trains run on time.

A SPIRITUAL RECKONING

There is for all a kind of spiritual reckoning in which we are invited to look at the meaning of our lives. This cannot be avoided, though it can be delayed. I would not recommend this unless you like sitting in huge empty corridors for days on end. Just accept that you are loved by those who meet and greet you; there is no need to be afraid. Imagine you are being interviewed for a responsible position and the interviewing panel has your CV before them. They know the absolute truth of your life and, though you may try, you cannot deny one iota of it. The spirits you now face are at the right hand of God. They are evolved souls whose duty it is to guide you into the next phase of your eternal life. Anger, remorse, sadness, self-pity or even joy, for that matter, carry no weight here. Before these spirits only your truth may be spoken. Yet they are in no way a threat to you, they are there purely to explain your position to you. As you hear the serenity of their benevolent voices, you will instantly know that you have reached the antechamber of eternity. Your soul will recognise the experience, for you have travelled this way many times before.

DESTINY

Your destiny in the world of spirit has been decided before you entered it. You yourself created it by the way you conducted your life on earth. As a general rule, the average individual has nothing to be concerned about. If you loved your family and were decent, though no better than the rest, then look forward to more of the same. From your brief interview with the higher spirits you will most likely proceed by some form of transport to your destination. What you find there will be of your own creation. It may be a beautiful villa overlooking a shimmering silver sea and inhabited by friends and family that you thought were dead. But there is no death.

For those whose lives have been wasted, or worse, there will now be an opportunity to reconsider. There are spiritual leaders in the next world who offer those souls who seek to repent and progress all the help they need to do so. No one is excluded. No one is a lost cause. But no one can expect to be transformed by magic; spiritual progression is earned by individual effort. All that a spirit is required to do to atone for a wasted life is seek guidance and act upon it. Mere words are useless. Expressing sorrow is pointless. There is but one way towards the light of God's love and that is through personal effort. In my heart I pray that you will understand this. It is the truth, God's truth, and you alone are responsible for your eternal life. No one can forgive you your sins – you own them, they are you. They are you in your true colours and God sees you as you too will see yourself in the kingdom that is to come.

THE DARK SIDE

There is an alternative offered to those who decline the self-less help of the enlightened spirits. There is the dark side, the kingdom of perpetual night. There you will find the angry and disaffected souls who, in their mistaken pride, refuse to accept the truth. Within these dark regions live the boastful sinners who scorn the idea that God loves them. But he does. And one day even the worst of these lost souls will look up from their self-perpetuating dungeon and reach for the light. Only when they do this can they be saved. God is waiting, forever and ever.

JUST REWARDS

For the vast majority there will be a period of due and just reward following transition. You have earned this respite from the struggle of human life by your actions on earth. However, you are building your home in the next world with every deed and thought you create while living this physical life. So the home you are heading for is yours in every sense of the word. It is, in effect, you.

Imagine that you are now creating and building yourself a house that you are going to live in. Your actions on earth form the material of this, your future home. If you use shoddy and inferior bricks and throw your house up in a slipshod, thoughtless way, it will not be a place of comfort, but an insecure ruin. You owe it to yourself to try to build the best house you can. Only you can build this house. It's no use praying and pleading to God to give you anything you have not earned. God is a good father to his children and loves them so much that He permits them to make mistakes so that they may learn by them and thereby progress towards perfection.

During this period of just reward, the spirit may rest and recuperate from a long and perhaps difficult life. Your spirit body will reflect your soul. In years you will be in your prime and so full of energy that you may wonder at your strength. You will find knowledge here, and there are those who will help you to learn about the many mysteries of God's kingdom. Time in this world does not exist. A thousand years may pass and you remain untouched, wrapped safely in the eternal love of God.

REJOINING LOVED ONES

Should your destined home not be with your former loved ones, you will be told why by the higher spirits. Each soul is made fully aware of the reasoning behind their spiritual location. It may be that your friends or former family members are too highly evolved to join you, or vice versa. For in the material world there are a number of extremely highly evolved spirits who have chosen to incarnate to lead humankind or otherwise influence events on earth. In their corporeal bodies these high entities are unaware of their spirituality. They are, however, fulfilling their earthly destiny and their presence on earth changes many things.

Generally those you have loved on earth will be joining you, or you will be joining them. Like attracts like on earth, and so it is in the world beyond. In time you may be invited to welcome an incoming son or daughter who is ready to join you in the glorious spiritual home that you and they have created. Your former pets will be there waiting, as they once did, for the loving touch of your hand. Our lives are enriched both on earth and in the world beyond by the love of our friends and family. It is God's good will that this be so, now and forevermore.

CONTACTING THE PHYSICAL WORLD

Should you wish to walk beside loved ones you have left behind, then you will be given the opportunity to do so. There are mediums in the spirit world too and they communicate with incarnate spirits on earth. You may become able to speak to or touch those who live on in their physical bodies. For you and for them the knowledge that life is eternal should be a great comfort. Mediumship brings that truth to both worlds and as such is one of God's divine gifts to his children.

REINCARNATION

In due course you will be given the opportunity to consider your personal spiritual progression. This may be through work in the next world. If you are so inclined, this could be with the lost souls who are seeking guidance. You may become a guide yourself, leading others, less evolved, towards God's love. Eventually you may decide that to progress yourself you need to reincarnate. There are higher spirits in the next world whose duty it is to help you plan your next life in a physical body. The lessons you need to learn will be discussed and you will undertake to learn them. At this point you will agree to address the karmic responsibilities you have accumulated. You may opt for a very difficult incarnation to counterbalance your negative karma. This will be your decision. You choose to progress at your own pace towards your ultimate destiny in the highest kingdom of God.

Before you can reincarnate, your life is planned, but it is planned by you. You have free will throughout your life, be it on earth or in the spirit world.

MY SPIRITUAL BELIEF

Ultimately we will all be at one with God in the highest sphere of His glorious kingdom. This is the divine plan. During my many years of meditation and enlightenment, I have been granted numerous insights into the nature of the world beyond.

When we are born into this physical world, we are born with a promise. This promise we have made to God who has granted us life on earth so that we, as the children of God, may grow closer to him. In this material world we are tested by God, who created us in His image. We are invited to fulfil the promise we made to God before we were born, but we have absolute free will to do so or not to do so.

You may view your lot in life as being little more than a terrible burden to be borne against your will. It isn't so at all. God would only give you that which you are able to bear and no more than is sufficient to meet your spiritual needs. Imagine that God is your father and you are His child. It would be an unkind father indeed that let his child wander into utter destruction, would it not? God is your father and He will not permit your immortal soul to be destroyed.

Yet He would be a poor father if He just lifted his child up out of harm's way each time that child was threatened. How then would the child learn? How would that child recognise the right path when each time it set foot upon the wrong path, Father reached out and rescued it from harm? You can see then that our God loves us so much that He permits us to sin and to walk in the valley of the shadow of death. Be strong and walk the straight road of righteousness into God's glorious kingdom. You can see the light, you recognise the truth; accept nothing less from yourself and walk forward with hope and joy in your heart. I have seen visions of the kingdom of God, and there is only ultimate peace awaiting us in the next world.

WALKING THE WALK

You may be thinking, It's all well and good for him to talk, he's a success, but what about me, what about my terrible life? Let me tell you what my spirit guides have explained.

God recognises your needs on earth and they will be met. All that you require to fulfil that promise you made before you were born will be given to you. However, you may try to avoid your duty and seek to wallow in the sins of the flesh.

God will let you do this, it is your life and you have to find
the pathway to paradise yourself.

So how do I find my pathway to the kingdom of God? So
you should ask, and you will find it, believe me. People may
have told you to have faith in God. I say to you, have faith in
yourself, you are a child of God. You may feel you have no
hope of doing anything worthwhile in this world. You may
think you are just a failure who can't win. But you are wrong
to think such things. You have it within yourself to be that
which you promised to be before you were born to this earth.

Let me teach you how I was taught to walk the walk.
Talking the talk is a waste of time, any fool can do that. 'I
believe, I have faith, I trust' – so what? All you are really
doing is putting the responsibility for your life onto some
invisible being that you refer to as God. Then when things
go wrong you can blame him. On your knees crying out for
help isn't the way to find your true pathway into the light, is
it? So get up, look around and make yourself do something
positive with your life.

I know how hard it is when there is no money, but I never
cried about the times when the going was tough. I was being
tested. We are all being tested as we walk forward. Sitting
down and moaning that God has dealt you a bad hand in
life's game of cards is no way to win. Only you can lose the
game by not trying. There is a saying that fortune favours the
brave, so be brave. Why not? What have you got to lose by
trying as hard as you can? You know that God is within you,
so have faith not in an invisible being called God but in yourself. The divine being we call God couldn't care less what
you believe, it is what you do with your life that matters.

There will be those reading this book who are physically
or mentally incapable of doing a great deal of work in this
world. Yet even the most disabled among us has a wonderful
role to play in God's divine plan. The gift of a smile when all
around know you are suffering is a beautiful thing. The light
of love in your eyes as you see those who care for you brings
with it joy. The gentle touch of your hand will never be

forgotten by those whose life you share. No matter how ill, how injured or how physically incapacitated you may be, have faith in your own self. To your own self be true and the pathway into the kingdom of God's love will open before you as surely as night follows day.

To all who read these words I say this; you are a child of God and it is your duty to walk the way into the truth and the light. Never be afraid, though you walk through darkness and death; you are being tested. Be strong and face all adversity with faith in your own self.

My thoughts are with you. May you find your glorious road into the light of the kingdom of God. It is your kingdom.

Further Reading

Bill Anderton, *Meditation: A Piatkus Guide* (Piatkus, 1999)

Judith Chisholm, *Electronic Voice Phenomena* ('An Teac na Pol' Rossenagreena, Glengarriff, County Cork, Eire)

David Conway, *Magic: An Occult Primer* (Jonathan Cape, 1972)

Joe Cooper, *The Mystery of Telepathy* (Constable, 1980)

Cassandra Eason, *Cassandra Eason's Complete Book of Tarot* (Piatkus, 1999)

Cassandra Eason, *Psychic Awareness: A Piatkus Guide* (Piatkus, 1999)

Harry Edwards, *A Guide for the Development of Mediumship* (Con-Psy Publications, 1996)

Kahlil Gibran, *The Prophet* (Penguin, 1991)

Eric Harrison, *Teach Yourself to Meditate* (Piatkus, 1993)

Linda Mackenzie, *Inner Insights: The Book of Charts* (Creative Health and Spirit, P.O. Box 385, Manhattan Beach, CA 90267, USA, 1996)

Ena Twigg with Ruth Hagy Brad, *Ena Twigg Medium* (W.H. Allen, 1973)

Index

READING THE FUTURE
A step-by-step guide to predictive astrology
Sasha Fenton
ISBN 0-7499-1607-9
£9.99 pbk

THE PSYCHIC EXPLORER
A down-to-earth guide to six magical arts
Jonathan Cainer and Carl Rider
ISBN 0-7499-1685-0
£10.99 pbk

MAKING THE GODS WORK FOR YOU
The astrological language of the psyche
Caroline Casey
ISBN 0-7499-1924-8
£9.99 pbk

A COMPLETE GUIDE TO PSYCHIC DEVELOPMENT
Over 35 ways to tap into your psychic potential
Cassandra Eason
ISBN 0-7499-1775-X
£9.99 pbk

YOUR PSYCHIC POWER
And how to develop it
Carl Rider
ISBN 0-86188-880-4
£8.99 pbk

ONE LAST TIME
A psychic medium speaks to those we have loved and lost
John Edward
ISBN 0-7499-1979-5
£9.99 pbk

AS I SEE IT
A psychic's guide to developing your sensing and healing abilities
Betty F. Balcombe
ISBN 0-7499-1320-7
£9.99 pbk

YOUR SPIRITUAL JOURNEY
A guide to the river of life
Ruth White
ISBN 0-7499-1903-5
£8.99 pbk

WORKING WITH GUIDES AND ANGELS
Ruth White
ISBN 0-7499-1605-2
£8.99 pbk

ASK YOUR ANGELS
A practical guide to working with angels to enrich your life
Alma Daniel, Timothy Wyllie and Andrew Ramer
ISBN 0-7499-1520-X
£12.99 pbk

THE ANGELS WITHIN US
A spiritual guide to the 22 angels that govern our lives
John Randolph Price
ISBN 0-7499-1914-0
£12.99 pbk

CHANNELLING
What it is and how to do it
Lita de Alberdi
ISBN 0-7499-1892-6
£8.99 pbk

CHANNELLING FOR EVERYONE
*A safe, step-by-step guide to developing your intuition and
psychic awareness*
Tony Neate
ISBN 0-7499-1720-2
£8.99 pbk

CHILDREN AND THE SPIRIT WORLD
A book for bereaved families
Linda Williamson
ISBN 0-7499-1773-3
£8.99 pbk

CONTACTING THE SPIRIT WORLD
*How to develop your psychic abilities and stay in touch
with loved ones*
Linda Williamson
ISBN 0-7499-1596-X
£8.99 pbk

Piatkus Guides
are lively authoritative introductions to the world of mind, body and spirit. Written by experts and packed with practical illustrations, they are the ideal books for exploring a wide range of subjects.

CELTIC WISDOM
Andy Baggot
ISBN 0-7499-1866-7
£5.99 pbk

THE ESSENTIAL NOSTRADAMUS
Peter Lemesurier
ISBN 0-7499-1868-3
£5.99 pbk

CRYSTAL WISDOM
Andy Baggot and Morningstar
ISBN 0-7499-1873-X
£5.99 pbk

FENG SHUI
Jon Sandifer
ISBN 0-7499-1870-5
£5.99 pbk

Piatkus Guides

TAROT
Cassandra Eason
ISBN 0-7499-1872-1
£5.99 pbk

MEDITATION
Bill Anderton
ISBN 0-7499-1871-3
£5.99 pbk

PSYCHIC AWARENESS
Cassandra Eason
ISBN 0-7499-1932-9
£5.99 pbk

REIKI
Penelope Quest
ISBN 0-7499-1935-3
£5.99 pbk

KABBALAH
Paul Roland
ISBN 0-7499-1957-4
£5.99 pbk

Piatkus Guides

COLOUR HEALING
Pauline Wills
ISBN 0-7499-1933-7
£5.99 pbk

MAYA PROPHECY
Dr Ronald Bonewitz
ISBN 0-7499-1959-0
£5.99 pbk

TIBETAN BUDDHISM
Stephen Hodge
ISBN 0-7499-1867-5
£5.99 pbk

ANGELS
Paul Roland
ISBN 0-7499-2020-3
£5.99 pbk

SHAMANISM
Gordon MacLellan
ISBN 0-7499-2023-8
£5.99 pbk